CITIZEN AND CHURCHMAN

CITIZEN
AND CHURCHMAN

by

WILLIAM TEMPLE
ARCHBISHOP OF YORK

LONDON
EYRE & SPOTTISWOODE, LTD.
14, 15 & 16 BEDFORD STREET
W.C.2.

First Published . . . *1941*

PRINTED IN GREAT BRITAIN FOR
EYRE AND SPOTTISWOODE (PUBLISHERS) LONDON

CONTENTS

INTRODUCTION

THE purpose of this series, as was said in the Introduction to the former volume, is "to help thoughtful Christians to be at one and the same time stronger in faith and more thorough in thought." That former volume—*The Two Moralities*, by Dr. A. D. Lindsay, the Master of Balliol—was described as a "little classic." I am conscious of great rashness in contributing to the series its immediate successor, more particularly because I am following in some respects a similar line of inquiry.

I wish to express my thanks to my secretary, Miss Dorothy Howell-Thomas, for converting the whole of my manuscript into typescript, and my special gratitude to my friend and colleague in this enterprise, Canon A. E. Baker, for many valuable suggestions and for preparing the Appendix which may make the book more useful to discussion groups or study circles.

WILLIAM EBOR

BISHOPTHORPE,
    January 13, 1941

It may be useful to begin with the last question. Recent political thought, from the sixteenth century onwards, has followed the lines traced out at the Renaissance. The new interest in Latin and Greek, especially Greek, literature of the classical age dominated the situation. Plato and Aristotle worked out the principles of political life and had no occasion to make reference to a Church as something other than the State, whether another aspect or function of a single society or another society altogether. When the Renaissance writers made their new start, breaking away from the medieval tradition, they took the great Greeks as their model. At first the breach with medieval thought could not be complete; Bodin and Hobbes have a good deal to say about the Church.

I

But attention to it steadily diminishes. It reappears in, for example, MacIver's *The Modern State* as an illustration of his contention that the State is not identical with the Community, and that there are human interests for which provision must be made through associations distinct from the State. This is something. But far from being a return to the distinctively Christian philosophy of the State, it is in reality a mile-post marking the distance away from it which thought has travelled. For what MacIver does is to classify the Church with voluntary associations generally and allow it to make for itself what place it can in the life of a Community of which the governmental organ—the State—is religiously neutral.

The Renaissance was in one aspect the proclamation of their autonomy on the part of several departmental activities in rebellion against the sovereignty of religion or theology. The Queen of Sciences was dethroned and nothing was put in her place. Politics proclaimed its autonomy in action when the agents of Philip the Fair kidnapped the Pope—Boniface VIII —at Anagni. It proclaimed its autonomy in theory when Macchiavelli published *The Prince*—concerning which the most illuminating consideration is that men debate to this day whether it is rightly described as cynical or as idealist. That book completely ignores all commonly accepted moral principles as guides to political action, and so far seems completely cynical; yet its goal is the national unity of Italy whereby the misery and bitterness of unending strife, bickering, and warfare may be ended. Macchiavelli is a true

2

idealist, but an unprincipled idealist. That is an inevitable result when Politics acknowledges no superior. The other departments of human activity asserted a similar autonomy; so that now because "Business is Business" the ease with which we can produce wealth is become a hindrance to producing it at all; "Art for art's sake" means that an artist's business is to express himself without regard to the question whether he has a self worthy or even fit to be expressed; and Education is at last recognised as the training of Personality at a moment when no one dares to say what is the function or destiny of Persons, except Communists and Fascists who alike degrade them into Robots.

The reason why the Greek philosophers had no theory of Church and State is not that they were secularist; Plato, at least, strove hard to find the religious foundation for politics. But the religions with which they were familiar did not claim, in any sense comparable with the Christian claim, to base their belief and practice upon a divine Revelation. Christianity, with Judaism from which it sprang and Mohammedanism which declined from it, is unique in this respect. The Jews have maintained their separation from all the nations among which they have been scattered, and have thereby become a political problem of the first magnitude. The Moslems until recently established theocracies, in which there was little or no tension between Church and State because the Church—the organ of the Revelation—was supreme. In Christendom there was tension to the point of extreme persecution while the State was supreme; for the agents of the State saw or felt that the new religion contained a serious threat to that supremacy. Then, as the Church grew in strength and the cohesion of secular society was declining, the great compromise was reached. Constantine proclaimed "the peace of the Church," gave to the Church an official recognition, and thereby purchased from its officers and members their support for the State and its authority. They had, indeed, in great measure given this before; for they recognised in the State a God-appointed agency for the maintenance of civil order. But their loyalty had been sorely tried by persecution, and to the Emperor who secured them against this they very naturally, but calamitously, offered in return a loyalty which gratitude rendered almost servile.

When the State was very weak, a strong Church could still lead society in resistance to attack. But when both Church and State were strong the tension revived. The political history of the twelfth and thirteenth centuries—the "Golden Middle Age"—is dominated by the Titanic struggle between Empire and Papacy. Where the most brilliant figure of the Middle Ages, Frederick II, failed, none could hope to succeed. The Papacy triumphed; and by its triumph and the steps taken to secure it, became corrupted. The Pope was established as an earthly prince, relying for his political treasury upon the religious contributions of the faithful. His sacred status was irretrievably compromised. A cry rings through many generations for reform of the Church in head and members, till the urge for reform at last broke through the barriers and achieved far more than its purpose; for it secured religious organisation freed from many corruptions at the terrible cost of breaking Western Christendom into fragments.

Thus in the period of Renaissance and Reformation we watch the Church's loss of moral and spiritual authority, then its disruption into a number of schisms, each claiming the authority which could only belong to the united body, none succeeding in exercising it. It was partly because of this that the various departments of life, hitherto organised, at least in theory, under the sovereignty of Theology and by principles which it supplied, were successful in asserting their autonomy. They have now worked out its results in the chaos of the modern world.

Yet all the time, and with increasing energy since the middle of the nineteenth century, the Church has proclaimed that she alone has the Gospel of salvation, and that all other departments of life owe by right an allegiance to that which she protects and fosters; for to her, as she claims, is committed the Revelation of God and of His will for man, in conformity to which the only true welfare of men can be found.

It is this claim to possess a Revelation, at once unique, final, and universal, which makes the Church a perennial source of difficulty to any State which does not avowedly accept that Revelation as the guide of its own action. At one time the State in England made such an avowal. It did not very greatly modify its conduct in consequence, and Churchmen so much valued the avowal as to condone, in most cases, the inconsistent conduct. It has been an ironical consequence of the secularisation of the State, that it gives the Church a certain new freedom to insist on its own principles in contrast with those apparently adopted at one time or another by the State. The growing distinction between Church and State may make it more difficult for the Church to permeate the State and direct it from within; it makes it easier for the Church, as a consciously distinct body, to impinge upon the State and influence it from without.

If all the citizens of a country were convinced Christians, who resolved that their country should be governed in accordance with Christian principles, there could be a completely Christian State. That condition has never been realised; indeed it never will or can be. What we have, and may expect that we always shall have, is a community made up of citizens who range from convinced faith to equally convinced atheism, and among believers from a maturity in faith amounting to saintliness to a puerility appropriate in children but devastating though frequent in adults. In such a community the State can be little other than neutral.

This leads to inevitable difficulties. For it is clear that the State acts for the community as nothing else does. It has a universal authority; and it is supplied with force for the maintenance of its authority. In the sense in which it exercises authority over its citizens, it is subject to no similar authority to which it is either expected or obliged to submit. It is

6

sovereign. But those of its citizens who profess the Christian faith believe that they have received a divine Revelation, which declares the character and purpose of God and, by consequence, the way of life for men. As this Revelation is divine, its authority is higher than that of any earthly State, even though it should be a world-state; it should control the State, yet the State (as we saw) must be almost neutral in respect of it and can give it little more than formal acknowledgment.

The distinctive enterprise of the Middle Ages was the effort of the Church, as repository and trustee of the divine Revelation, to control the State. It was in principle a laudable enterprise; but it rested on a false expectation of success within history and was so led to adopt methods which betrayed the very nature of the Church.

It was a laudable enterprise, because men and nations ought to obey the law of God and the Church ought to know and proclaim that law. So far as the nations recognised a spiritual authority in the Church, and the Church was content to exercise an authority which was truly spiritual, the result was good. And this was so far the actual fact, that the victory of the Papacy in the long struggle with the Empire may be regarded as more advantageous to Christendom than its defeat would have been, or even a sustained balance of mutually hostile powers.[1]

But though the enterprise was laudable, and Christendom owes much to Gregory VII, Alexander III,

[1] See appendix to this chapter on the Medieval Experiment.

7

and Innocent III—even perhaps to Innocent IV and the others who finally broke Frederick of Hohenstaufen and his heirs—yet it was misconceived. We must work and pray for the coming of God's Kingdom on earth; and every new assertion of God's authority over His world is sheer gain; yet we must also recognise that the Kingdom cannot come in its perfection within the period of human history and under its conditions. For while history runs its course, even though all mature persons should be deeply converted and purged of self-interest, yet new individuals, new generations, would still be coming on the scene, looking out upon the world from themselves as its centre, estimating the importance of all things by the question how their own interest is affected, and generally spoiling the harmony. History is not leading us to any form of perfected civilisation which, once established, will abide. It is a process of preparing the way for something outside history altogether—the perfected Kingdom of God. In that work of preparation we have to make rough places plain; but as soon as this is done, places previously plain are found to have become rough.

In order to secure the quick returns for which men are so eager and in which, apparently, God takes no interest at all, the Church set itself to secure its own authority over States (of course in the name of the divine revelation entrusted to it) by the same methods whereby States maintain their authority over citizens or sovereigns over vassals. The Popes built up political alliances; they mobilised armies; they employed coercion. But this was a desertion and betrayal of their commission. We see it now as we look back. We need not blame them. Probably the experiment had to be tried once before men would recognise that it both was, and was bound to be, a failure. Also it had this measure, surely very great, of justification, that Christianity is bound by its very nature to be totalitarian. It claims, and must claim, to control the whole of life. And nothing else—neither People nor State—can be allowed to advance a similar claim. It was not the ultimate aim or fundamental principle of the Hildebrandine Reformation which was at fault, but the method.

With the failure to which that method inevitably led there came the break-up of the unity of Western Christendom, first of its intellectual and political unity in the Renaissance, then of its religious unity in the Lutheran-Calvinist Reformation. The intellectual unity had been relatively complete; there were "schools of thought", but within one framework. That unity, however, was to some extent due to the persecution and suppression of heresy—an application in this sphere of the false method characteristic of the whole enterprise. The religious unity also was relatively complete, though vitiated by its reliance upon the same support. The political unity had never been complete. England from an early date claimed to be an "empire"; the French Crown acknowledged no allegiance to the Emperor, who was the theoretical focus of European unity. In fact such political unity as was achieved in practice was less due to the political structure itself than to the reverence felt for the Papacy; and this could not survive without great loss the "Babylonian Captivity" at Avignon and the Schism which followed. When there were two Popes, and kings chose on political grounds the Pope to whom their reverence should be given, that reverence could be little more than formal. The ending of the Schism by the Council of Constance could not restore the Papacy to that exaltation which enabled the great Popes of the twelfth and thirteenth centuries to impose some real unity upon the turbulent chieftains who occupied the thrones of Christendom.

In countries which accepted the Reformation various principles were adopted. Luther sought to make the Prince *summus episcopus*, and entrusted to him the ultimate control of the Church. He assumed that the Prince would always be a Christian. Hence the subjugation of the Church to the State in Germany, and its peculiar difficulty in face of the Nazi revolution; for it can be contended with a fair show of probability that Hitler is, on Luther's principles, entitled to the control which he exercises. Of course it is also true that Luther would have loudly denounced the mode and direction of that control, and (being never unduly concerned about consistency) would have contemptuously repudiated it. In Scandinavia the connexion between Church and State is very close. In Sweden the King prescribes the texts on which sermons shall be preached on many Sundays in the year; but the submission is not all on one side, for the Synod has the right to veto an Act of Parliament dealing with a moral issue, and has exercised that right within the last twelve years, as the late Archbishop of Upsala informed me.

In the Reformed Churches the example of Calvin at Geneva led to attempts at theocracy, or the subordination of the civil to the ecclesiastical authority. Hence the tyranny of the Covenanters in Scotland. The English settlement had Reformed or Calvinist features in its Articles of Religion, though the extremer doctrines of the Reformed tradition were avoided; on the political side it was Protestant or Lutheran, though here again the extreme position was avoided, except in the later years of Henry VIII and the reign of Edward VI. Elizabeth did not reassert Henry's claim to be Supreme Head of the Church, contenting herself with the title of Supreme Governor; and though the Crown and Parliament wielded authority over the Church even in matters of worship, the Church displayed at crucial moments a spirit of independence, and had in its hierarchy and convocations a means of expressing its judgment and of directing, even if extra-legally, its own life.

This sketch of medieval developments and of the variety of principles adopted at the Reformation is offered here simply as evidence that this problem of the relations between Church and State is perennial in Christendom and is inherent in the nature of both.

If the Church were a purely spiritual society and the State had purely secular functions, it might be possible for the two to work side by side without collision or friction. But of neither is this true. The Church has its secular aspect; indeed listeners to debates in the National Assembly of the Church of England have sometimes complained that it seems to have no other. That is not a fair inference even from the Assembly's debates. But it is a fact that the primary business of the Assembly is legislative, and the legislation desired by the Church concerns mainly such questions as Clergy Pensions, Dilapidations, and so forth. But this fact shows that the Church has concerns which bring it within the sphere where the State has undoubted authority; for all property is held subject to law, and the State is the law-maker. A purely monastic Church would still be subject to the State in respect of its tenure of its monasteries. The only way to escape the authority of the State is to own no property at all; and that would be a deprivation of means to do spiritual work such as it would be madness to incur unless the alternative were a compromise of fundamental principles. The Church is rightly subject to the State in respect of its tenure of property.

The State, in its turn, must not be confined to the purely secular sphere. Its primary duty is to maintain that order which makes possible the free and unimpeded activity of its citizens. But this is not all. As Aristotle observed long ago, having come into existence to maintain life, it continues to exist in the interest of the good life. It concerns itself, and increasingly, with the welfare, including the moral welfare, of its citizens; and here it is on ground which is the proper province of the Church. How are the functions of the two to be defined and correlated?

The Churchman is also a citizen. That is universally true. And the simultaneous membership of the two societies creates some problems for every Christian. The citizen may be also a Christian; the relationship when stated from this side is not necessary nor universal. But from this side also problems arise when the statesman or civil servant is also a Christian. How far is he entitled to act in his public capacity on principles which many members of the public do not accept?

The relations of Church and State are bound at all times to give rise to problems. To some extent, as we shall see, those problems arise within each of the two as well as between them. This rather complicates than alleviates the problem; but it also suggests its inevitability in any society which has been brought into the Church or even in which the Church has been planted.

APPENDIX TO CHAPTER I

The Medieval Experiment

For the sake of any reader who has not had the opportunity to become acquainted with the great attempt to order human life in the earlier Middle Ages I offer an amateur's outline sketch.

The later Roman Emperors—from Diocletian onwards—divided the Roman Empire into two parts. The Eastern Empire, based on Constantinople, lasted until 1453. The

Western Empire fell before the barbarian attacks in 476, when Romulus Augustulus resigned the "useless purple" and Odoacer became ruler of Italy—soon to be succeeded by Theodoric, founder of the Gothic Kingdom of Italy. But the memory of the great peace remained and throughout the years of chaos men's minds were haunted by the recollection and the hope of a really ordered life. It was the achievement of Charlemagne to reconstitute for a moment the political unity of Western Europe; and the Pope—Leo III—recognised this when he, uninvited, put a crown upon the monarch's head on Christmas Day, A.D. 800, in St. Peter's, at Rome. Charles, however, divided his empire among his sons, and a period of disintegration followed.

The Holy Roman Empire begins to appear with the election by the Franconian and Saxon magnates of Henry the Fowler to be their king—A.D. 919. He consolidated his kingdom, and at his death in 936 Otto I came to the throne. Otto first established his authority in Germany and then secured recognition as overlord of Italy. He was crowned as Emperor by Pope John XII in 962. Five years later he secured the coronation of his son Otto II, and thus both ensured the permanence of the Empire and suggested a hereditary character for its chief.

At about this time the Papacy sank into great degradation. The elections to the Papal throne were "controlled by a ring of greedy and corrupt Roman nobles, conspicuous among whom was the fair but dissolute Theodora and her daughters Marozia, wife of the Marquis Alberic I of Camerino and the less important Theodora the younger."[1] The ambitions of this family reached their zenith when Octavian, son of Alberic II, being already secular ruler of Rome, became Pope as John XII (955). But an influence was spreading through the Church from Cluny, where a new monastery had been founded in 910. The descendants of Otto had concerned themselves to improve matters in

[1] Tout: *The Empire and the Papacy*, p. 30.

14

the Church, and this led to a great advance when Otto III nominated Gerbert, who assumed the name of Sylvester II (999). The co-operation of Emperor and Pope continued on the whole till Henry III was won to the Cluniac programme of reform and nominated his cousin Bruno who took office as Leo IX (1048). The whole movement reached its climax when Victor II, who succeeded Leo IX, died in 1057, and was followed to the grave one year later by Stephen IX. After an illegal election, Hildebrand secured the election of Nicholas II (1058), himself becoming Archdeacon of Rome. He was the main director of Papal policy from that time onwards, and in 1073 became Pope Gregory VII.

Pope Gelasius I (492–6) had laid down the doctrine that Emperor and Pope are alike supreme, each in his own sphere; this became the formula of the Imperialist party. Gregory VII makes the Pope alone supreme: "If Peter's successor has the right of judging and unbinding in heavenly and spiritual matters, how much greater is his right over earthly and worldly things."[1] He exhibited, for a time at least, the supremacy which he claimed when he kept the Emperor Henry IV waiting in the snow outside the inner gate of the castle yard—fasting and clothed as a penitent —at Canossa (1077).

The struggle of Empire and Papacy went on with varying fortunes till near the end of the thirteenth century. Its high lights are (1) the quarrel and reconciliation between Frederick Barbarossa and Alexander III, with the scene in the Piazza at Venice (1177) when, just a hundred years after Canossa, the Emperor threw himself at the feet of the Pope; (2) the reign of Innocent III (1198–1216), who came nearest of all the Popes to realising the Hildebrandine dream—the Pope to whom our King John resigned his crown to receive it again as a papal fief; (3) that Pope's choice of Frederick II as Emperor, and the brilliant reign of Frederick (1212–1250)

[1] Quoted by Coulton: *Studies in Medieval Thought*, p. 175.

in perpetual conflict with successive Popes; (4) the extinction of the line of Hohenstaufen, to which both Barbarossa and Frederick II belonged, in the defeat and death of Manfred (1266) and Conradin (1268); (5) the supreme expression of Papal claims by Boniface VIII (1294–1303), his kidnapping at Anagni and his humiliation—not at the hands of an Emperor representing the unity of Europe on its civic side, but at the hands of the purely nationalist King—Philip IV, the Fair—of France (1303). With that event the great days of both Empire and Papacy ended, and the scene was set for the new national states under their vigorous dynasties, with France, Spain, and England in the leading parts.

The story when told in detail seems to be one of conflicts and wars due to rival ambitions. That is part of the truth. But when we leave the details and look at the picture as a whole we see a great aspiration towards unity wrecked by failure to find a true adjustment between Church and State, Papacy and Empire. At that time men thought in feudal terms which corresponded to the logic commonly accepted. In the realm of thought men looked for Universal as governing principles. Under each Universal as *summum genus* were grouped its main sub-divisions, the various *genera*; beneath these again were the different *species*; and to these belonged the individuals. So in political life the King was at the head of the nation; the nobles "held of" the King; the lower ranks "held of" the nobles; and at the base of the pyramid were the villeins or serfs. How was the unity of Christendom itself secured? Imperialists, or Ghibelines as they were called, adopting the formula of Pope Gelasius I, insisted that the Kings "held of" the Emperor who himself "held of" God. But the Papalists, called Guelphs, taught that only the Pope held directly of God, and that the Emperor held of him. In proof of this they cited the act of Leo III in putting the crown on the head of Charlemagne, and the coronation of Otto I by John XII.

16

There were real principles at stake. Hildebrand (Gregory VII) saw clearly that the spiritual should control the material, that faith should govern life. But he misconceived the nature of the spirit in its relation to life generally; he accepted the view that man's spirit can rightly be coerced. He relied mainly, it is true, on so-called spiritual censures. But excommunication carried with it in those days an alienation of all "faithful" people. When Henry IV sought absolution at Canossa, we know that it was not chiefly with a view to receiving the Sacrament, but with a view to ending the political disaffection of his subjects. This so-called spiritual censure was in fact a political weapon.

Innocent III, the greatest of all Popes, followed this line of action by calling on princes to fight his battles. When his protégé, Frederick II, came to his full power, successive Popes, and especially Innocent IV, had to develop the normal resources of political action, including finance, in order to resist him. After Frederick's death they won, and the greatness of the Empire was destroyed. But the Popes had compromised the spiritual character of the Church in winning its political victory.

All of this was implicit in the very method of Hildebrand. His goal was right, but (like the Communists of our day, whose aim, so far as it is universal fellowship, is also right) he chose a method which was bound to frustrate his hopes of ever reaching that goal.

On the other side the great Emperors, especially Frederick Barbarossa, Henry VI, and Frederick II, though of course they had personal and dynastic ambitions, were inspired by a hope of universal order and peace secured by strong government. It is noteworthy that the stricter Franciscans attached themselves to Frederick II, and that Dante took his ideals sketched in *De Monarchia* largely from the achievements of that brilliant figure. They were right to resist the Papal intrusions in the purely political field. For politically the Pope was an Italian princeling; he claimed to manipulate

17

the forces of all nations through the obedience of their kings, but in fact he could only call on those whose kings found it convenient to support him. Consequently his political action was bound to be, as it was, a source of disorder and war rather than of order and peace. If Christendom was to be a political unity it must have a centre possessing political strength.

But the aim was too vast. The Roman Emperors with their legions had maintained the *Pax Romana*: the Holy Roman Emperors never had that measure of force at their disposal nor the unquestioning loyalty of vassals. The career of Frederick II illustrates the difficulty. He was the German King; but he resided, when not on Crusade or Campaign, chiefly in South Italy and Sicily. Without the mighty organisation of the Roman Army and without modern communications, the problem of control was insoluble. The future did not lie with either Empire or Papacy, but with the national states slowly coming to maturity. When the Papal claims reached at once their apogee and their catastrophe in Boniface VIII, the deadly foe was a King of France.

We may take A.D. 1300 as the year when the great medieval experiment finally ended. For about two centuries after that we watch the decay of medieval Europe. The dream of unity was fading; the nations were finding unity each for itself as the authority of the Crown over the feudal nobility was increasingly established. After A.D. 1500 we enter on the "modern" period, now reaching its close. The will of our Henry VII is entirely medieval in spirit. The figure of Henry VIII is entirely modern. He takes the stage with Francis I of France and Charles V of Spain, who added to the crown of Spain the crown of the Holy Roman Empire. For a moment the Empire seemed again to be a reality, and we find the troops of the Holy Roman Emperor sacking the city of the Popes in 1527. But the revival was hardly more than a flash. Charles divided his far-flung realm between Ferdinand of Austria and Philip II of Spain. Thenceforward the Imperial title is little more than an adventitious dignity of the essentially nationalist House of Austria, though it lingered till Napoleon abolished it after the battle of Austerlitz in 1805; the head of the House of Hapsburg then became Emperor of Austria.

The Papacy underwent in the Counter-Revolution a revival almost as remarkable as that of the Cluniac or Hildebrandine Reformation. It increasingly abandoned its activities as a small Italian principality and in consequence recovered much of its spiritual authority and influence. But the political and financial ambitions of the Popes from 1250 till 1550 had cost it the allegiance of the northern nations, and it never again became a centre of universal authority such as was wielded by Innocent III.

CHAPTER II

The State

WE cannot profitably discuss the relations of Church and State, or of men's duties as Churchmen and as citizens, until we have a tolerably clear conception of what we mean by the two words Church and State for this purpose. It is even possible that if we can rightly define our terms the proper relation between them will be evident and the problem theoretically solved. There has of late been a great deal of speaking and writing about the nature of the Church; the very fact of our divisions and the controversies to which they give rise have ensured this. But there has been little discussion except among philosophers concerning the nature of the State. This is not because all men are agreed about it, but rather because all inhabitants of any one area are subjects of the same State, and they are not driven to choose between rival theories of it. But there are rival theories; and the war between Germany on the one side and Great Britain with her allies on the other is in part a conflict between two of them.

There are two main aspects of any theory of the State; one concerns its relations to its own citizens, the other its relations to other States. These two are distinct but not independent one of another. It has been a conspicuous vice of recent political thought

and action to suppose that no nation is interested in
the internal affairs of another. It is, no doubt, both
true and important that no nation should interfere
by military force or by diplomatic action (which is
usually the same thing in essence, in spite of the velvet
glove drawn over the iron hand) in the internal affairs
of another. But the reason for this is that such interference is almost certain in the long run to defeat its
own object by creating resentment, not that no nation
has a legitimate interest in the internal affairs of its
neighbours. The Russians and indeed all Marxists
know better than that! It is not possible for any
State to adopt one set of principles for internal affairs
and another for external; for what determines its
action in either case is its understanding of human
life in general. If the State represents Christian
citizens, it may often fail to act by Christian principles;
but it will not (so far as the citizens are truly Christian
and effective in their influence) steadily act on principles opposed to the Christian view of life. Some of
our politicians and diplomatists have suggested that
it was necessary, before May 15, 1939, to watch and
see whether the Nazis would apply to other States
the principles on which they had seized and maintained power over their own fellow citizens. That is
a false suggestion. The only real question was not
whether they would do this, but when. It may well
have been right to wait, for considerations of expediency might hold them in check for a time, and the
German people might throw off the tyranny. There
is always an immensely strong case for postponing

the action which precipitates war. But there could never have been any reasonable doubt what would be the principles followed in their foreign policy by the men who were guilty of the Beuthen telegram, the Reichstag Fire Trial, and the 30th of June 1934.

It is clearly impossible to review here the many various theories of the origin and nature of the State.[1] This book is written from an avowed Christian standpoint, and this at once rules out some varieties.

No Christian, and indeed no Theist, can admit that the State is entitled to an absolute allegiance. Such an allegiance is due to God alone; and He is the Father of all men. All States, like all other parts of the created world, exist to do Him service and to give Him glory. Similarly, no Christian can admit that the individual citizen exists solely for the service of the State. He is first and foremost a child of God, destined for eternal life in fellowship with God. He has a dignity higher than that of the State; his kings and rulers share this with him, in virtue of the common humanity. The State exists to serve the common man.

In the English Coronation service it is highly significant that all which concerns the King's royalty is set within the Holy Communion service, as is the ordination of a minister. A deacon is ordained after the Epistle, a priest after the Gospel; a bishop is consecrated, a king is anointed and crowned, after the Creed. When the anointing, investiture, and crowning are complete, and after homage has been rendered to the crowned king seated on his throne,

[1] See my *Christianity and the State*, Lecture II.

22

the order of Holy Communion continues exactly as in any village church; and he who was seated as the crown of earthly majesty was set upon his head is kneeling as he receives, like any of his subjects, the sacrament of the Body and Blood of Christ. In the greatest thing, king and pauper are on a level. No theory of Government which loses sight of this can be compatible with Christianity.

There are two main ways of regarding the State, and each contains much truth. One way is to regard it as a construction which men have set up. This is true in greater or less degree of every state as regards its institutions. They have been largely shaped, as generations pass, by reform or revolution. This way of regarding the State finds its most characteristic expression in the many forms of Social Contract. One philosopher used this as a device for providing a theoretical basis for absolutism; Thomas Hobbes conceived the social contract as established between the citizens, who agreed to transfer certain of their natural rights and liberties to the Sovereign. The Sovereign, not being a party to the contract, could not break it. To him each citizen owed unqualified obedience on pain of breaking his contract with his fellows. But the Sovereign was independent of the contract and superior to it, in spite of the fact that his sovereignty was due to it. In this, however, Hobbes is unique. Other theories, as propounded by Calvinists in France in the sixteenth century, by Locke in the seventeenth or by Rousseau in the eighteenth, use the contract to define and limit the authority of the State, and by its

23

definition to make clear the conditions under which the State forfeits its authority so that rebellion becomes morally permissible or obligatory.

It is now generally recognised that theories of a Social Contract cannot in any case be more than mythological; probably this was the intention of their several authors. There never was a moment when a contract was made. But a contract between Sovereign and people is implicit in their relations to one another. This aspect of the truth is very naturally most emphasised by those who for one reason or another wish to curtail the power of the State or to censure its action. It is therefore the philosophy of revolutionaries, or of those who, for one reason or another, are discontented with the Government and wish to modify or overthrow it. Because of this desire they fasten on the aspects of the State which disclose it as a constructed, almost manufactured, fabric, which can be remodelled by hands similar to those which constructed it.

Those who are more content with society as it is fasten their attention on the complementary truth that it, and the State as the organ of its unity, have grown up in a long process of development, being shaped from time to time in accordance with men's needs as experience directed. They justly criticise the Social Contract theories on the ground that these give a false suggestion with regard to the development of society and the State; for their suggestion is that the problem has been to construct a social unity out of a mass of individuals each moved by his own interest

24

alone. Hobbes states this explicitly. But this inverts the historical fact. The initial datum, so to speak, was not a mass of isolated individuals who were driven by the misery of their isolation and their ceaseless clashes of interest to coalesce into a society; the initial datum was a very close-knit society in which the individuals had very little freedom of action or choice; custom was all-controlling. Progress has come, not by the fashioning of unity out of multiplicity, but by the creation within the social unity of liberty for its component individuals and groups. As this process goes forward the social unity may be imperilled. The State, on such a view, represents the specific interest of the whole over against those of its own parts. Thus it becomes the appropriate source of Law, of which the essence is its universal applicability. The primary function of the State is to make and enforce Law governing those aspects or departments of life in the society concerned, which are appropriately controlled by universal rules. Most fundamental among these is that degree of order which is indispensable to effective freedom of choice and action in individuals or functional groups. If private citizens or bodies are allowed to use force against other citizens or bodies, freedom is imperilled; if they actually use it, freedom is destroyed. Anything like a "private army" is a contradiction of the civilised State. The State itself is entrusted with force in order that it may prevent the use of force by anyone else; if its own force is known to be sufficient, no one will resort to force from anger, ambition, or any other personal motive; in fact it may truly be said that the State is entrusted with force in the hope that, as a result, there will be no use of force within the community at all, except such disciplinary use of it in the subordinate communities (families, schools, etc.) as illustrates in its own sphere the same principle—force the instrument of law.

If this is true, it is at once evident that no formula could be more misleading than the definition of the State as Power. The State is essentially the source and upholder of Law, and its sphere is all that is appropriately regulated by Law. It is not its own end. It is an organ of the community, indispensable to the continued existence of the community but entirely subordinate to it. Its end is the welfare of the community. And the community consists of persons. It is not an entity existing somehow in detachment from its members; it is essentially those persons united in social unity. Consequently we cannot form a theory of society or of the State until we have formed a conception of human personality.

We are approaching the matter as Christians, and therefore need not now consider what may be said about human personality by those who do not take the Christian standpoint. If we are Christians we believe, amongst other things, the following: (1) God is supreme, and no authority may be set up parallel with His: that is the first of the Ten Commandments; (2) God is the creator of the world, whose providence guides history and whose judgments are discernible in history; (3) God is the Father of all men, whom

He has created that they may have eternal fellowship with Himself; (4) Mankind has not responded to the divine call and claim, but has pursued a self-centred existence, each following his own will in preference to God's; (5) God has taken upon Himself the burden of evil resulting from this sin of mankind, and in Christ—supremely in His death—has shown forth the depth of love which was the motive of creation and thus completes the creative purpose by redeeming the created but vitiated race of men; (6) the ingathering of the harvest of the redemption wrought in Christ goes forward in the historical process through the Church and is in fact the source of all meaning in that process.

If the Christian standpoint is adopted, it is clear that human personality has a status, worth, and dignity quite independent of the State, and superior to that of the State itself. The State was made for men and women, not men and women for the State.

Men and women, however, do not exist as isolated units. The Original Sin of man, which is his self-centredness, shows itself not only in each setting up his will in the place of God's, but by consequence in his preference of his own interest to that of his fellows. It is, indeed, precisely a failure to love God with all his heart and his neighbour as himself. He is not willing to count for one among the rest; and only if he is won to set God, not himself, in the centre can he become so willing. He needs a "Copernican revolution." If the earth is taken as the centre, the sun is only one of the heavenly bodies, and it, with all the planets, is conceived as moving about the earth. So each man, making himself the centre of his own view and estimate of the world, thinks of God (if at all) as one of the beings who impinges on his existence, and of other men as deriving their importance, for him at any rate, from their relations to himself. But when the sun is recognised as the centre of the solar system, the earth takes its place as one of the planets revolving about the sun. So when a man recognises God as the true centre of life, he takes his place as one among God's children.

Men see quite clearly that they are by nature members of the human family, or of some section of it, and they recognise the consequent obligations. The commonly accepted moral principles are all affirmations of this membership. Men exist in families, in nations, and in other social units; they have no existence apart from these. A man's relation to his parents is not accidental; he is not an independent being who might have been born of other parents; he is in the heart of his being their child. We are social through and through; it is thus that God has made us, and our self-centredness is an offence not only against Him and our neighbours, but against our own real nature.

These considerations bear upon our conception of the State in two ways—over and above the fundamental principle that the State exists for the citizens, not the citizens for the State. First, the individual owes allegiance and obedience to the State because it is the representative and effective organ of the largest and most inclusive community to which he belongs. It is its organ for present action, the custodian of its tradition, the trustee for its future; for the nation is not only a fellowship of contemporaries, but a partnership of present with past and future. All that is purely temporal in the citizen, including his animal life, is rightly subject to the State which acts for the whole community, including, of course, himself. The State may not claim the subservience of his conscience[1] or demand that he act contrary to it. His spiritual integrity and his fellowship with God take precedence of his citizenship. But the range of activities which are in themselves spiritually neutral, and derive spiritual or moral quality from the way in which they are exercised in face of changing circumstance, is within the just control of the State so long as conscience is not violated. The State may take his goods in taxation; it may demand that he change his occupation, as when it conscribes men in its armies; it may thrust him into a service involving certain death. Its right over him is limited only by his conscience and his obligation to live in the spirit of fellowship with God.

The State which possesses this right is not an alien power; it is the organ of the community and itself exists to serve the community, or, in other words, the citizens. So far as it becomes in practice one group of citizens maintaining itself in power by oppression of the citizens, it becomes a tyranny,

[1] By "conscience" I mean the individual's conviction concerning right and wrong. Sometimes it is a reflective judgment, sometimes an emotional reaction, sometimes an intuitive perception. At its best it combines all three.

betrays its own nature and function, and is legitimately thrown out of the seat of power by successful rebellion. (Here is the strong part of Social Contract theories.)

Secondly, the State, whose primary service to the community is to uphold its order, is not thereby doing violence to the citizens against whom it enforces the law, but is holding them to conduct expressive of their true nature. For the individual who asserts his will against the law is exhibiting the self-centredness which is his essential sin. Not every sinful action is a crime, nor is it desirable to make it so; but in a well-ordered State every crime is also a sin. The State which punishes criminals, thereby checking criminal tendencies and enlisting the self-regarding motives in support of justice, is helping men and women to be true to their real nature as God created it. Very few citizens are so established in virtue as to be able to dispense with the support of the law and its penalties without moral deterioration. It is from the vantage ground secured by the Law that we make our response to the Gospel.

But the State does not, and cannot, stop short at the maintenance of order. Indeed the very conception of "order" expands as it becomes relatively secure. At first the maintenance of order may mean little more than the prevention of riots or of physical violence. But when personal immunity from attack is secured, the question arises whether cut-throat competition is not in the same category of disorder as the cutting of throats. It can reasonably be claimed that the evil conditions in factories immediately after the Industrial Revolution were acute forms of disorder, and that Lord Shaftesbury's Factory Acts were passed for the establishment and maintenance of reasonable order in that sphere.

Yet this transition, though easy and natural in itself, is epoch-making in its consequences. The State had, indeed, concerned itself with that area of life in the Middle Ages, through the Charters of the many Guilds, which it issued. The Privy Council, during the period of Charles I's personal rule, tried to regulate terms of employment and dismissal; and this interference with the rising *bourgeoisie* in their exploitation of the new opportunities opening out before them was a greater factor in the Parliamentary opposition to that monarch than has been generally appreciated. Archbishop Laud was undoubtedly high-handed in the method of his action; but his main concern in this field was to protect the interests of the poor.

The triumph of a Parliament in which labour had no representation put an end to the hated interference of the Crown. John Locke, the philosopher of the Whigs, added the rights of property to the elementary human liberties which the Government was pledged, by his version of the Social Contract, to protect. In the eighteenth century there was, no doubt, much interference with freedom of trade under the guidance of the "mercantilist" theory; but there was little attempt to control the relations between capital and labour except in the way of suppressing riots, rick-burning, machinery-smashing, and the like. Later the horrors disclosed by Parliamentary inquiries into factory conditions stimulated the public conscience to such effect that the State took up again its earlier function in ways appropriate to the changed conditions.

But, as has been said, this revival marked the inauguration of a new epoch. The State, entering again its former field under a specifically moral pressure, found itself impelled in the direction of regulating the welfare of its citizens in general. Its concern with education was at first a part of its concern for those pauper children whose labour was being shamefully exploited in the new factories; and its first enterprise in this field was to found, at Kneller Hall, Twickenham, the first training college for teachers;[1] these teachers were to teach in Poor Law Schools. Owing to a change of Government, these schools were not provided at that time and the whole scheme failed. None the less, this was the thin end of a very thick wedge. In 1870 the State made universal education compulsory and provided "Board Schools" in the places where there was not already a school maintained by the Church of England through the National Society or by the other religious agencies through the British Schools Association. Education, hitherto a sphere of voluntary and in fact of religious activity, thus became a sphere of State activity.

All the conditions of modern life, so favourable to central administration, favour the extension of State activity. The modern Probation System started as

---

[1] Of which my father was Principal.

the Police Court Mission of the Church of England Temperance Society. We are actually witnessing an extension of the concern of the State to include the whole welfare of Youth. In such developments we see at work the principle which, if allowed free play unchecked and unbalanced, produces the Totalitarian State. And without more ado we may readily admit that the State, as organ of the community, may rightly be concerned with all that takes place in the life of its community. The urgent question is how far, and in what way, it can recognise the equal concern of other agencies, and accept them as its own instruments for fulfilling its purpose. To this we shall return.

Hitherto we have been dealing with the State in its relations to its citizens. The view which we take of these must affect our view of its relations to other States. If we start without the Christian pre-suppositions, the State or the community for which it acts will appear as a whole of which the citizens are merely parts. (The word "merely," which is commonly illegitimate as involving the begging of questions, is here in place and is intended. For the citizen is, on any theory, a part of the national community; the question is whether he is also something more than this). If the citizen is a mere part, his interest is properly subordinate to that of the whole. Moreover, inasmuch as *ex hypothesi* there is no God for the State to serve, the State becomes an absolute. Sovereignty is then its essential attribute—Sovereignty over its subjects, Sovereignty over against other States. For the exercise of this Sovereignty force is indispensable. So we arrive at the maxim "The State is Power." If that be granted, the method of exercising this power is a matter of expediency only. Concentration camps, in which persons, not condemned for any offence legally defined but regarded as dangerous or suspect by agents of the State, are confined for indefinite periods, are then perfectly legitimate. They may be unwise, as causing disaffection, or wise as removing the disaffected from all opportunities of influence. And whether wise or unwise, depends entirely on circumstances; they may be wise at one time and unwise at another. There can, if this view of the State be adopted, be no moral condemnation of them.

Similarly, in the absence of Christian or at any rate of Theistic pre-suppositions, the State confronts other States as an absolute Sovereign. It owes no allegiance to any authority higher than itself. In dealing with another State, it will consider the interest of its own citizens only—understanding thereby their material or economic, not their spiritual interests. It will not be bound by any considerations of morality. The action of Communist Russia in Finland, or of Nazi Germany in Poland, Denmark, and Norway, is fully justifiable by the principles professed by those States. Internal tyranny and external aggression must alike be expected from States which are regarded by their subjects and their administrators as absolutely sovereign. Yet there is no logical ground for regarding the State in any other way except faith in God.

We have only to observe the articles in even our most reputable newspapers to see how far we have ourselves surrendered to this essentially atheistic conception of politics. In 1915 I returned from a brief visit to the United States at the time when Italy was hesitating whether or not to enter the war. The first issue of *The Times* which I saw contained a leading article to the effect that in deciding this question the Italian Government must consider solely the interests of Italy. Very likely this was good diplomacy and well calculated to assist the decision of the Italian Government to enter the war on our side. But in its implication that the duty of each State is to consider only the interest of its own nation, it was atheistic. Of course the State must consider those interests, but not without reference to the Law of God; the nature of the moral obligation of the State will concern us later.

If on the other hand we accept the Christian presuppositions set out above (pp. 26–7) a totally different result follows. We have already seen that in place of the conception of the Power-State we are led to that of the Welfare-State. Similarly inasmuch as, on this view, the essence of the State is its function as the fountain and upholder of Law, possessing force not because its essence is Power but because Law must be enforced, the State is true to its own nature when it directs its international policy towards the establishment and maintenance of international law, even though this involves (as it must) the abrogation of its own sovereignty. For on this view, only God is

Sovereign in his own right. The State is Sovereign contingently and conditionally; its essential function is to secure the rule of Law in accordance with Justice. It fulfills itself in submitting to any authority which may be set up by itself and other States for the regulation of their mutual dealings. The State, in short, is a servant and instrument of God for the preservation of Justice and for the promotion of human welfare so far as this can be done by universal enactment or through opportunities created by universal enactment.

Thus the State has a moral and spiritual function. It is not possible to divide human interests into two categories—the material and the spiritual—and to assign the former to the State, the latter to the Church. The State, as entrusted with the administration of Justice, is plainly concerned with some aspects of morality. But in addition to this—being obliged to recognise that its citizens, for whose welfare it is in part responsible, are spiritual beings—it has at least an indirect spiritual function. Caesar-worship, and its modern revivals, have that measure of justification; and if the spiritual life could be regimented without grave detriment, the regulation of religion by the State would be tolerable, if the State were truly universal, that is to say a World-State, and if it accepted the Divine Revelation as its standard. But in fact the State is disqualified for the regulation of religion by two considerations. In the first place the State is geographically limited and the life of the spirit knows no such limitations; this is fatal to the claim of the national State to control religion. But if we suppose that objection removed by the emergence of a World-State, the inappropriateness of this World-State for the task of controlling religion is evident. For the second consideration referred to above is the essential spontaneity of truly spiritual life, which makes regimentation abhorrent to it. And while a national State, basing itself on national traditions, may exercise a control over religion which is not felt as intolerably irksome, the control of a World-State would inevitably impose such fetters as to stifle all real spiritual life.

The spiritual function of the State, then, cannot be rightly exercised through direct control of religion by Acts of Uniformity and the like. These are an inheritance from an age when the distinction of functions as between Church and State was far less clearly discernible than it has now become. The English State has in practice ceased to take steps of its own for the enforcement of those Acts, and leaves the Church to pay so much attention to them as a general respect for law and a regard for spiritual vitality combine to suggest as appropriate. It begins to be recognised in practice, and had better be plainly avowed, that the spiritual function of the State is not to regulate religion but to make free scope for it and to uphold the regulations made for its expression by the religious associations themselves.

All this follows from the nature of man's spiritual life, without any regard to a special divine Revelation. If such a Revelation has indeed been given, then those who accept it are not members of a religious association which they constitute by the act of their own wills in joining it, but are incorporated by the movement of the Divine Spirit into a fellowship which is properly called Church—a word which means "belonging to the Lord." The State may recognise the Church, treating it for its own purposes either as a voluntary association which it is not, or as a divine creation such as it claims to be. If its citizens are in a large majority sincere Christians the latter course may be adopted. The result will be the only sound form of "Establishment"—not a control of religion by the State, but an agreement on the part of the State to recognise the divine authority of the Church and to lend its aid in the upholding of the order of the Church so far as this may be required by the Church itself. But in that case the State must also see to it that the Church does not overstep its own proper function or call upon the State to exercise on its behalf coercion in the spiritual sphere, where coercion is out of place.

So far we have been considering the spiritual function of the State. When we turn to its moral function we find a more complicated situation. The State is, in practice, the people who administer it. What is their duty when acting on behalf of the nation? On the one hand they are trustees for the people—not only for their contemporaries but for the generations yet unborn. On the other hand they are the agents and spokesmen of their own nation in its place in the whole family of nations. Much depends on the extent to which the nation is unanimous upon any issue. The State can rightly take action for a unanimous community which it would be wrong to take if great numbers of citizens dissented. We must not either personify the nation and treat it as a moral agent in the same sense in which an individual is a moral agent; nor must we regard it as exempt from moral obligation. No general code for the ethical guidance of states can be drawn up. The ultimate moral principles apply to states as to men and are unchanging; but their application depends on many factors, including the ethical outlook of the citizens. The way in which, on Christian principles, the conduct of a nation or state is to be moralised will claim our attention later when we have considered the nature of the Church in outline, as we have considered the nature of the State.

CHAPTER III

The Church

FROM the standpoint of the State, as we have just now seen, the Church is liable to present the appearance of a voluntary society, because there is no legal compulsion to belong to it. But in the estimation of its members the Church is not a voluntary association. It is not constituted by men deciding to form it or, later, to join it. It is the creation of God, and men become its members under the impulse of the Holy Spirit through the sacrament of Baptism. Indeed, one of the advantages—(there are disadvantages also!)—attached to the practice of infant Baptism is its clear expression of the truth that we do not make ourselves Christians. The fact that we are Christians is not due to any act on our part; it is due to the act of God in Christ through the Holy Spirit. We may thereafter be good Christians or bad, loyal or apostate, but the fact of incorporation can be no more undone than our membership of our families. By birth I came into the world as a child of my parents; by Baptism I was brought into the Church as a "member of Christ." My parents could care for me or neglect me; they could not prevent my being to all eternity their child. My fellow Churchmen could teach me or ignore me; they could not alter the fact of fellow membership. I could respond to my parents' care or rebel against it; I could not cease to be their son. I could submit to the influence of the Holy Spirit in the Church reaching me through such members of it as had dealings with me or I could repudiate it; I could not alter the fact of my membership.

There is much here that is difficult, and the analogy between Church and family can be pressed too far; for the family relationship is rooted in the natural order as Church membership is not. My physical sonship is in itself a fact which carries other implications with it, but is itself unaffected by them. My incorporation into Christ is something which is formal only, and therefore potential only, until it is actualised in spiritual life and experience. The form is not unimportant; one of the commonest mistakes is to suppose that because "form without content" is empty, all importance comes from the content. That is not so. There can be a block of marble which is artistically shapeless; but the form or shape has more to do with the beauty of a statue than have the physical properties of the marble.

So far as there is a controversy about the importance of "form" at this point, it arises from uncertainty or difference concerning the nature of "spirit." We so commonly contrast "material" and "spiritual" that we easily suppose matter and spirit to be mutually exclusive opposites. For Christians this is certainly not true; indeed Christianity is the most materialist of all the great religions. Other religions achieve spirituality by turning away from matter—calling it illusory or in other ways attempting to ignore it or to build up an esoteric life in detachment from it. Christianity conceives the spiritual as a power controlling the material and becoming actual in that control, so that in its understanding of the world matter exists to be the vehicle of spirit, and spirit is actual in its exercise of control over matter.

It is certainly true that a material form or vehicle, designed by spirit for its own expression, may survive when there is no spiritual purpose or meaning which uses it for self-expression. When this happens a sacrament degenerates into magic, and the fear of magic which holds many people off from the use of sacraments, finds abundant occasion in the history of Christendom. But to reject sacraments on account of this fear is to fall into error on the other side, and to suppose that the spiritual element in religion can exist and energise without material embodiment. Whatever may be true of other worlds than this, in this world such detachment of spirit from matter is impossible. Even physical emptiness (as in the Holy of Holies) or silence (as in a Friends' meeting) is a negative physical symbol. We never escape from the physical; to attempt it is either to let the physical run riot with resultant moral catastrophe or to impair its usefulness by excessive mortification. The central declaration of the Gospel is "The Word became *flesh*"; and our hope is set, not on a purely spiritual immortality, but on a Resurrection of the body.

But it is clear that this principle commits us to a way which is indeed strait and narrow. It is so easy to multiply ceremonies and be punctilious in their observance; it is so easy, at least for many people, to indulge in emotional aspiration or mystical day-dreaming; and it is so very hard to dedicate the whole of life. But this alone is true worship—the giving to God of body, soul and spirit ("ourselves, our souls and bodies") with all that they need for their full development, so that He may take and use them for His purpose.

The Church, which is the witness of this truth to the world and the sanctuary of such worship, must needs be sacramental and make use of sacraments. And if the Church itself is sacramental, it is so appropriate as to be indispensable that admission to it should be by a sacramental rite. No doubt, if a choice had to be made, it would be better that a man should be a loyal disciple though unbaptised than that he should be baptised without ever becoming a loyal disciple. But why should the choice be made? Let sacraments be used, and used for what they are— "certain sure witnesses and effectual signs of grace and God's good will towards us, by the which he doth work invisibly in us, and doth not only quicken but also strengthen and confirm our Faith in him" (Article XXV).

By Baptism, then, not as an isolated ceremony but as a true sacrament expressive of God's redeeming love and gracious welcome, we are made members of the Church. The mode of our admission to it is expressive of its own nature. That nature is two-sided, as everything sacramental or indeed everything human must be. It is the fact of man's natural two-sidedness which makes possible a Church composed of human beings. Man is both animal and spiritual. On one side he is the most fully developed of the animals; but if that were all, he would present, and know, no problems. Upon him is stamped the Image of God; he is capable of that communion with God which is eternal life. But here again we find two-sidedness; for the Image of God in man is blurred and distorted. How or why this should be so is a question too large for discussion here. The fact is certain. Man, capable by his nature as God made it of communion with God as the author, centre, and goal of his being, does always in greater or less degree conduct himself as though he were himself his own beginning and end, the centre of his own universe. His "sin" is not a mere survival or disproportionate development of animal tendencies, or an inadequate development of rational control. It is a perversion of reason itself. His capacity for divine communion is become a usurpation of divine authority. The worst, most typical sin, from which all other sin flows, is not sensuality but pride.

Now the Church is the Body of Christ; and its members—the limbs of that Body—are sinful human beings. All that is said about the Church must keep both parts of that paradox in view.

The Church is the Body of Christ. Yet the writers of the New Testament never regard it as coming into existence at the Nativity—still less as being born or inaugurated at the Feast of Pentecost. It was there before Christ came to redeem it. As Dr. Goudge

44

often said, there are in the Bible two doctrines only
—God and the Church, God and the People of God.
Everything falls under one of those two; and God is
known chiefly through His dealings with His people.
From before the time when history is distinguishable
from legend there was a community conscious of a
commission to bear witness to the One True God.
If it has any human founder, that founder is Abraham.
We watch the vicissitudes through which this people
was disciplined and trained. In all that happened its
teachers, the prophets, bade the people trace the hand
of God. From a conviction that for them there was
but One God, whatever deities might preside over
other nations, this people was led to believe that the
God who had chosen them for His own was indeed
the God of all the earth.

This was, perhaps, first proclaimed by Amos;
certainly Amos proclaimed it. It was the faith of
Isaiah and Micah and Jeremiah and the author of
Deuteronomy. But until the Exile it never gripped
the whole people. Then came what seemed the great
calamity; Judah followed Israel into captivity. It
appeared that the reforms of Josiah in accordance
with the prophetic teaching and that of Deuteronomy
had come too late. They were too late to save the
whole people; but they may well have played their
part in saving the remnant. For when the nation went
into Exile the prophetic faith was the faith of a
minority. In the nation that returned it was in sole
possession. For those who had not accepted or who
lost this faith were merged among the nations and

45

did not come back. The Exile was a sieve and sifted the grain from the chaff. From that time onwards Judah was a Church-Nation or Nation-Church. Its faith was its constituent principle.

Yet as before the Exile the Prophets had seen that the whole people would be unworthy of its destiny, which would be achieved only in the Remnant, so at the moment of Return the great Second Isaiah perceived that the whole even of the returning Remnant would not be worthy. The "Servant of the Lord," who is at first the whole people, dwindles to a section and shrinks at last to a single individual upon whom the Lord lays the iniquity of all.

So it came to pass. The true Servant of the Lord was born. But He was not welcomed or followed by more than a few; and at the last those few deserted Him: "all the disciples forsook Him and fled." In perfect obedience to the will of God and quite alone the Lord went forth bearing His own Cross. In that moment He was in His own person the whole People of God, the true Israel. But by His bearing of the Cross, by the love and obedience both manifested and perfected in total sacrifice, He put forth a power drawing all men to Himself. Those who are thus drawn are united to Him as the branches in the vine, incorporated into Him as limbs in the body, so that the People of God, the true Israel, is thenceforward all those of whatever race or nation who have heard and received the Gospel.

Men do not constitute the Church by joining it. It was constituted at first by God in calling Abraham

46

from his home upon his journey to the unknown; it was reconstituted by God in Christ, who was at the critical moment the whole Church or People of God and who gathers to Himself the elect—those to whom the Gospel comes and who are able to answer its call. It is the "one man in Christ Jesus" who, as new members are incorporated into the Body, grows towards "the measure of the stature of the completeness of the Messiah."

This Church—the very word, kirk, means "belonging to the Lord"—is that of which the Apostles use their glowing phrases: "a glorious Church without spot or wrinkle or any such thing"; "an elect race, a royal priesthood, a holy nation, a people for God's own possession"; "the pillar and ground of the truth." What is its relation to the ecclesiastical organisations known in history and in our own experience?

First let us try to free our minds of a natural but disastrous misconception. The term "Church History" is commonly used with far too narrow a meaning; it is used for the record of ecclesiastical assemblies, doctrinal controversies, and the like. Its real meaning is "The story of the impact of the Gospel upon the world." Thus the Abolition of the Slave Trade, and later of Slavery, was a signal achievement of the Church, the People of the Lord. If I were asked to point to any great achievement of the Church in England in the twentieth century so far as it has gone, I should point without hesitation to the reform of our penal administration. It cannot be entered in the Official Year Book of any denomination. But most of the work of the Church is done, not by ecclesiastical officials nor under the direction of ecclesiastical committees, but by members of the Church who do the ordinary work of the world in the inspiration of Christian faith and in a spirit sustained by Christian prayer and worship.

So regarded, the historical record of the Church is less remote from its scriptural description. Yet the paradox remains. And it was already present in primitive times. The Church of Corinth, considering its size, was as fertile of disquieting symptoms as the Churches of Rome or of England at any period of their histories. The paradox is part of the Scriptural deposit, not a result of later deterioration. Still, it is true that those who know anything about the Church of the ninth and tenth centuries, before the Hildebrandine Reformation, or about the Church of the fifteenth century just before the Lutheran, Calvinist, and Ignatian Reformations, find conspicuous difficulty in applying to it the glowing phrases of St. Peter or St. Paul. And those who face the actualities of past or present must agree with Dean Inge in refusing to "suppose that the forms which Christianity has so far assumed—Jewish-Christian Messianism, the paganised Christianity of Western Catholicism, the fossilised Christianity of the East, the disrupted and fissiparous Christianity of the North—are any better than caricatures of what Christ meant his Church to be."[1]

What then is the relationship between the actual and the ideal or true Church? Or—to put the same

[1] Inge: *Speculum Animae*, p. 21.

48

question in other terms—what is the relationship
between the Church as historically organised and the
Kingdom of God for the coming of which we are
taught to pray? This second form of the question is
useful because it reminds us how deep the paradox
goes. For it is present within the conception of the
"Kingdom of God" itself. That phrase means
primarily the Reign or Sovereignty of God, and there
is evidently a most important sense in which that is
a permanent and unalterable fact. We never escape
from the Sovereignty of God; His law always operates.
Yet in another sense His Sovereignty is incomplete so
long as the operation of His law is manifest not in
the obedience of His people but in the destruction
which it brings upon the disobedient. In an earthly
State, the law is upheld when under its provisions a
thief is imprisoned; but the real object of the law is
not that thieves may go to prison, but that men may
not steal. The law is most effective when there is no
occasion to call it into play. So the Rule, Reign, or
Sovereignty of God, which is manifest only in the
calamities consequent on breaches of God's law, is as
yet imperfect. It is absolute, yet it is not the satisfaction of its own nature. The Kingdom for whose
coming we pray is manifest in the willing obedience
of God's people to His will; and to this the Kingdom
manifest in judgment is an indispensable disciplinary
means. So the Kingdom is in one sense always here;
yet for its coming in another sense we pray. Yet it
is one and the same Kingdom in two stages of self-
manifestation.

Now the Church in its true nature is the fellowship of the redeemed, who, being incorporated into Christ by Baptism and endowed with the Spirit as promised to the Messiah[1] for the doing by each of his share of the work of Christ, and nurtured through Holy Communion with the very life of Christ, move always and only under His will, veritable members or limbs of His Body. But such a Church is not actual at all and never has been. Its members are also members of the sinful world, and the sin of their own nature and of the world still infects them. The actual Church therefore is an arena wherein the Spirit of Christ, whose indwelling causes it to be the Church, is in conflict with the spirit of the world from which the members of the Church are drawn.

Moreover the Church in its corporate life is on one side an association with worldly interests of its own. Unless it is to consist solely of hermits, its members must have property with all the cares and interests which this involves; but also if it is to have the means of effective action the Church corporately must hold some property with those same cares and interests. Then a very difficult situation arises. What are the administrative officers of the Church to do if a conflict arises between perfect loyalty to Christian principle and sacrifice of the means whereby Christian influence is exerted? Of course no question should arise if the balance were as clear as that way of putting the question suggests; but in practice it is not so. It is more likely to arise in this kind of way: the

[1] Compare the Confirmation Prayer with *Isaiah* xi, 1-4.

Church we will suppose holds certain funds which supply the meagre income of a large number of missionaries—priests, doctors, teachers—in a heathen country. Those funds are in the form of State bonds. The State embarks upon a policy, not flagrantly evil, but tinged with acquisitiveness and widely popular, and there is a party in the State disposed to urge the confiscation of the funds owned by the Church. Is the Church to risk the ruin of its missionary work by denouncing that policy? I submit that only a cynic or a fanatic can regard that question as quite easy to answer. The difficulty is not that of choosing between right and wrong, but of deciding where in all the complex of circumstances, right actually lies. For it can hardly be said that the Church ought to denounce the State every time the State acts on less than absolutely Christian principles; indeed the State has actually no right to act on those principles unless the whole body of citizens desires this. But if the Church is bound to acquiesce in less than absolute Christian principle as the basis of State action, it is evident that the choice when to intervene is very difficult. Moreover the Church consists of the same persons who are also citizens of the State; and if most citizens are members of the Church, there cannot be any very wide divergence between the moral outlook of the Church and that of the State.

So far as any demand is made for denunciation or protest on the part of the Church, it is usually a demand made by those who are led by their consciences to form a minority, and it is addressed not to the whole body of the Church but to the hierarchy. Now it can happen that members of the Government are Christian men; and it is by no means obvious that Christian men who are Bishops will have a more Christian view of, for example, Foreign Policy than a Christian man who is Foreign Secretary. They may be free from certain pressures to which he is subject, but they may be subject to others from which he is free; and if there is anything in this democracy we hear about, perhaps he ought to be subject to and guided by those pressures. It looks as if the Church had better get on with its missionary work and leave the State to do its own business.

Yet even that cannot be left to stand in that crude form as expressing the real truth of the matter. If under pressure from vested interests the State pursues a policy involving injustice or a plain denial of equal fellowship, the Church which silently acquiesces is rightly discredited. And as the experience of history proves that the temptation to acquiesce in a wrong course taken by the State is stronger and more persistent than the temptation to oppose the State on insufficient grounds, it is wise to encourage rather than to discourage such independent action.

Enough, however, has been said to show that inevitably, and not only because of the worldliness or supineness of ecclesiastics, the Church as a body corporate is entangled in the perplexities and relativities of this world. It has, moreover, often yielded disastrously to the resulting temptations. It is, in addition, peculiarly exposed to the temptation to "rationalise," as modern psychologists put it, and so prove to itself and suggest to the world that considerations of pure righteousness prompt the course of action which is incidentally so highly advantageous in a financial sense. Those who have a professional obligation to uphold moral standards need to be very specially on guard against rationalisation of that sort. Worldly cynicism is less nauseating than pious humbug! But the course of honest testimony to principle in this tangled world is very difficult and only possible where faith in God has really exorcised self-centredness and self-concern.

This apparent digression, dealing with the complexity of the Church's ethical problem, has aimed at showing how impossible is a clean-cut distinction between Church and world, and how easy is the lapse from a sane Christian estimate of the tangled situation to a worldly and unchristian acquiescence and even partnership in evil. The Church as represented by the Papacy fell into the snare set for it in the later Middle Ages. Accepting the Pauline and Augustinian identification of the Church and the Kingdom of God, the Popes had tended to regard service to the temporal interests of the Church as service to God, or any attack upon its temporal interests as an attack upon God. But, of course, the Church when it becomes a property owner or even a temporal State, stands on a level with all other property owners or States. If it is desirable to nationalise certain forms of property, such as minerals, the Church has no claim to treatment in its capacity as an owner which differentiates it from other owners. For the Church in its true nature has no concern with such things; its property is an instrument for the doing of its work. If it abuses that property, or employs it to the public detriment, it ought to be deprived of it equally with any other owner. Should the Church or some of its officials acquire status as a temporal principality, it comes under the law of nations. If a Pope is a Prince and wages war, it is no worse and no better to fight against him than against any other temporal sovereign.

The confusion which we are here condemning was very prevalent in the Middle Ages and often appears in modern discussions of Establishment or Dis-establishment. This latter is, properly speaking, of no interest to the Church. It is entirely a question for the State to determine whether or not it should associate itself with the Divine Society. If it wishes to do so, on terms which do not hamper the Church in the discharge of its own mission, this recognition by the State of the Sovereignty of God is naturally welcomed by the Church. But the concern of the Church must be the retention of its freedom to fulfil its own commission. Its members have not always observed this principle.

The acute intermingling of Church and world in the Middle Ages was a main cause of that disruption in the sixteenth century which we call the Reformation. For many generations the cry had been raised for a reformation of the Church "in head and members." Councils attempted it at Pisa, at Constance, at

Basel. The failure of these led to the great break-away. From that time onwards four main theories have been held concerning the relation of the Church to the Kingdom of God:

(1) *Roman.* The Church *is* the Kingdom. Most if not all of what seem to non-Romans the errors of Rome are intimately associated with this stark identification, which gives to an historical and in part earthly institution a claim to absolute allegiance.

(2) *Lutheran.* The Church is visible only in the preaching of the Word and administration of Sacraments; its members are known only to God. They are the elect. They are citizens of the Kingdom of God, but that Kingdom and with it the true Church will become visible only at the final consummation. This view involves an incapacity in the Church to guide the State. They have separate functions, and each is rightly supreme in its own province. The only occasion when the Church should actively resist the State is an intrusion by the State into the spiritual affairs of the Church.

(3) *Calvinist.* The elect may be sure of their own election though no man may know concerning another whether he is elect or reprobate. The congregation of the elect is the Church, the true "people" (*peuple* as distinguished from *populace*) in any realm or region. They should secure obedience to the Divine Law as widely as possible, and if they can control the machinery of the State should do so and use it to this end. Here the Church is an instrument for establishing the Kingdom, which is conceived primarily in

terms of obedience to the Divine Law. Hence arose
the inquisitorial tyranny of the Scottish Covenanters.
Hence arises the "Activism" of many American sects,
for whom the Kingdom of God is a social and
economic Utopia to be established by political means
under pressure from Christian citizens organised by
their Churches to vote the right "ticket."[1]

(4) *Orthodox and Anglican.* The Church as it exists
on earth is constituted as the Church by the presence
and activity within it of the powers of the Kingdom.
But these are partly hidden and confined by the
worldliness of those who are members of the Church.
The goal of its existence is the bringing of all men
into fellowship with God. The Orthodox Church
looks forward to an "apotheosis" of the whole
creation—"that God may be all in all." For this view
the Church has within it the "first fruits" of the
Kingdom. The Kingdom is in it as the statue is in
the marble block; it is often concealed by excrescences
and a purification is needed before it can become
apparent. But there it is; and it is in virtue of this
that the Church is the Church; indeed it only deserves
that name so far as those inner powers actually govern,
or in the technical sense of the term, "inform" it.
And its task is to win the world to acceptance of the
Gospel till Church and world are one—one altogether
not by conversion of the Church into an earthly State
but by incorporation of mankind into Christ.

[1] When Dr. Oldham issued a Questionnaire on the Nature of the Church
as part of the preparation for the Oxford Conference on Church, State, and
Community, one American professor opened his reply with the words: "It
is evident that the Church is a pressure-group." I know no phrase which it
would be harder to interpolate harmoniously into the *Epistle to the Ephesians.*

The function of the Church then is primarily to be itself—the People of God, the Household of the Lord, the Body and Bride of Christ. Secondarily its function is to win the world into itself. It is not a means to the Kingdom which can be discarded when the Kingdom is come; rather the coming of the Kingdom is the perfecting of the Church.

We may illustrate the nature of the Church as it exists now in the world by the figure of a draped lantern. It is only a lantern at all because the light is in it. Yet it cannot be a lantern and consist only of the flame which gives the light. The other material of which it is made—the framework and the glass sides—can perfectly serve the lantern's purpose of giving light. But if the glass is faulty or soiled, and if the whole is shrouded with a veil, the light will either be dimmed or else will not reach the outer world at all. So in the Church the true light shines because in it the Gospel is read and the Bread of Life is offered. If these be not done, there is no Church at all. But the world which looks on may never see the light because the lives of the members of the Church, including those who read that Gospel and offer that Bread, betray the treasure entrusted to them. To some extent this is always so; sometimes it is so to an extent which totally obscures the light. Yet the light is not extinguished; the Gospel is still read and what is offered, though by unworthy hands, is still the Bread of Life; therefore the Church is still the Church, though in its historical and local manifestation it is false to its true nature.

Consequently the Church itself puts these prayers into the hearts and mouths of its members:

"Keep, we beseech thee, O Lord, thy Church with thy perpetual mercy: and, because the frailty of man without thee cannot but fall, keep us ever by thy help from all things hurtful, and lead us to all things profitable to our salvation."

"O Lord, we beseech thee, let thy continual pity cleanse and defend thy Church; and, because it cannot continue in safety without thy succour, preserve it evermore by thy help and goodness."

"Lord, we beseech thee to keep thy household the Church in continual godliness; that through thy protection it may be free from all adversities, and devoutly given to serve thee in good works, to the glory of thy Name; through Jesus Christ our Lord."

"Christ also loved the Church and gave himself up for it; that he might sanctify it, having cleansed it by the washing of water with the word, that he might present the church to himself a glorious church, not having spot or wrinkle or any such thing, but that it should be holy and without blemish."

CHAPTER IV

The Interlocking of Church and State

IT is often urged that the Church should be completely independent of the State in order to bear its witness to the absolute claim of the Gospel with independence and fearlessness. From what has been already said it must now be evident that such independence is impossible. On the one side the State, rightly developing its own concern for the welfare of its citizens, undertakes activities which are within the province belonging to the Church. If the Church withdraws from these because the State steps in, it hands over channels of spiritual influence, such as schools and probation work, to secular forces. Yet it cannot claim complete control if the State provides the resources. Co-operation is therefore inevitable, and co-operation may involve some measure of compromise.

It is part of the evil of our religious divisions that the State cannot merely endow religious activities, exercising only such vigilance as would ensure that its bounty is not abused. If all citizens were members of one Church it could do this, if the citizens being also Churchmen approved; and this might well be an ideal arrangement. Thus all schools might be in practice controlled by the Church and financed by the State. Our divisions make this impossible. The task of adjudicating between the claims of rival sects would be impossible; indeed the quarrels of Christians in the past led many who were not unfriendly to religion to advocate a purely secular system of education as alone compatible with justice and smooth administration.

But there would be grave dangers in that apparently Christian State. If all citizens are Churchmen, and all those citizen-Churchmen are devoted Christians, the Kingdom is come and our problems are ended. But if Christian devotion fails, the coincidence of Church and State must become a source of evil. For the constituency of each being the same, it will be impossible for the Church to take a stand on a moral issue opposed to that taken by the State which represents exactly the same persons. It is indeed always true that the Churchman, unless he withdraws altogether from the world, is influenced in his outlook by the same forces which determine the mentality of his fellow citizens. But if at the times when he acts as a Churchman he is conscious of standing for something which many of those fellow citizens repudiate, he finds in that consciousness a call to his distinctive Christian witness. "What is everybody's business is nobody's business." It ought not to be so, but so it is—not so much because men are wicked as because they are limited in capacity. A man cannot do everything, so he does first what is specially entrusted to him; he may then find that his time and strength are all used up, and that he has none left for what is his business only because it is everybody's.

Here, it may be urged, the ministry of the Church has its function. The clergy differ from the laity precisely in this, that for them religion is their special business. The layman seeks in his religion the inspiration which will enable him to do in a Christian spirit work which can be done, and largely is done, by men of no religion; the clergyman finds in religion the work itself as well as the inspiration of it. This difference exercises a subtle and widely pervasive influence, so that there is liable to be a great divergence between the lay and the clerical outlook even where there is genuine Christian faith on both sides. Consequently it is quite impossible to leave the responsibility of Christian witness in respect of most practical problems to the clergy. They have not the requisite knowledge; but beside this, they have an outlook which is specialised in an irrelevant direction. None the less they have a real function in this connexion; it is, not to formulate policies, but to stimulate in the laity a sense of responsibility and remind them of the claims of their Christian faith in the various departments of life. But the actual leavening of the world's lump with the energies of the Kingdom of Heaven must be done by laymen. To some aspects of that task we shall return when we consider the inter-related obligations of Churchmanship and Citizenship.

As the State imposes upon the Church co-operation, and to that end some measure of compromise, by the mere fact that it conducts activities which fall within the Church's province, so the Church is of necessity subject to the State in so far as it functions as a corporation. It could be corporately free from the State if corporately it owned no property. Perhaps it would be best that it should secure freedom in that way, and finance its entire work by the free contributions of its members—if only they could be relied upon to contribute with great generosity and (quite as important) with unfailing regularity. But this must then be carried to the utmost limit. The Church buildings themselves must be privately owned on behalf of the Church by members of the Church. It is easy to see that in any community of less than perfected saints such a scheme must quickly break down and the authority of the State be resumed; for as soon as any dispute arose concerning the use of those buildings, the only referee would be the State, interpreting Trust Deeds through the mouth of its Judges. The great Scottish Church case is an illustration of this point. There was in that case no question of establishment. The Free Church was precisely that which had gone out from the establishment, leaving behind all its wealth, in order to obtain freedom. But it did not obtain it. When a question arose whether it had forfeited its newly acquired property, the free gift of its own members in the half century last past, this could only be decided by the Law Courts interpreting the basic documents of the Church. In its new constitution the Church of Scotland has attempted to make its freedom complete; and it may have done so; but it has done this only, if at all, by the device of securing from Parliament a

Declaratory Act. In that Act Parliament does not in any sense confer freedom on the Church; it recognises that the Church possesses freedom; and to that end it recognises the General Assembly as the competent and final authority for interpreting the constitution of the Church. Yet even so it seems that an aggrieved citizen might bring an action based on the allegation that the Assembly which promulgated some decision was irregularly constituted or summoned; and then it is hard to see how the Courts could avoid pronouncing on the validity or invalidity of the acts of that Assembly. Every citizen has and ought to have right of appeal to the Crown for lack of justice; consequently every extant corporation, including the Church or the corporate bodies which act for it, is subject to the State in so far as the State has authority to check it from acting *ultra vires*.

The Church on its side should not be fettered by these considerations in the ordering of its spiritual life; but it cannot simply ignore them. If to insist on some point of worship or discipline would involve the forfeiture of property held as a means of ministering to those who are too poor to provide for a fully equipped Church life among themselves, it is evident that a balance of advantage and disadvantage must be struck. It is all very well to say that the Church must maintain its freedom in things spiritual at all costs. But actual freedom to carry on spiritual work may depend upon the means of doing it; and the assertion of a principle may involve the loss of opportunity to act on that principle. No doubt, the

63

temptations of worldliness are at this point both subtle and urgent. In avoidance of them it is well to incline rather to the quixotic than to the over-prudent course of action; but prudence is a virtue and fanaticism is not.

Our countrymen have a rooted tendency to believe that the distinction between right and wrong is not only absolute in principle but evident in fact. This is a complete delusion, and a source of much moral blindness. In such a problem as we are now con-sidering, it is fairly easy to sketch an ideal relationship between Church and State for a community of Christian citizens who are in sufficient numbers devoted, wise, and sympathetic. The world is not like that. It is of great importance to have a clear conception of the ideal. But only when the ideal is actualised can any consistent course be followed without serious evil. This does not mean that in the actual world no one course of action is right; it means that the right course is to be found by striking a balance of goods and evils, and will be found to involve the foregoing of some goods, probably also the acceptance of some evils. The Church, in its historical situation and in its actual decisions, is bound to the relativities of all historical action as completely as anyone or anything else.

In this connexion it is of supreme importance to bear in mind two facts concerning our Lord: (1) He was God Incarnate and we are not. Not only were many actions possible to Him which are not possible to us as sinful individuals, but many were appropriate when done by Him which would not be appropriate if done by us. (2) In His human life He was unmarried, and truly detached from earthly ties. He had His own special mission, the specifically universal mission, for the discharge of which He must be free from all particular commitments and the obligations resulting from them. At first He directed His followers to practise a similar detachment, as in the charge to the Twelve before their first mission (St. Matthew x). But later, when the things concerning Him had fulfil-ment, He deliberately countermanded this: "But now, he that hath a purse let him take it, and likewise a wallet; and he that hath no sword, let him sell his cloke and buy one . . . for that which concerneth me hath fulfilment" (St. Luke xxii. 36, 37). He prepared His disciples for a change after the critical moment was passed; with the Cross and Resurrection His Kingdom would have come with power, and they were no longer to be apart from the world, bringing to it *ab extra* the divine act of redemption which is itself the revelation of God, but were to carry its power into the world as leaven that should leaven the whole lump. But that is to leave the sphere of the absolute for the sphere of relativity, of balanced decisions and of practical adjustments.

The loyalty of the disciple is still to Christ and His absolute demand; but that demand is to be fulfilled, not by isolation from the world but by the life of consecration in the world. In order that this may actually occur there is constant need of witness to the absolute claim, and God calls some to leave other responsibilities that they may devote themselves to that witness. So St. Francis was called to embrace poverty as a bride; and he let this be known and by his life challenged the consciences of others. But he never said that all other Christians must do the same. He never said that no good Christian could be a merchant, as his own father was, trading honestly but seeking a fair profit in his various transactions. The Church welcomed and honoured Francis. But when some of his followers appeared to say that all possession of wealth was wrong, the Church condemned them. This double action of the Church was manifestly right in both its parts.

Of course this argument could be twisted into a defence of ecclesiastical worldliness; and it is to be recognised that to live in the world yet in spiritual detachment from the world, is a harder moral task than to seek isolation from the world in voluntary poverty. It is a familiar thought that it would be for most of us easier to die for Christ than it is to live for Him. If we were confronted with the sharp choice —Renounce Christ or die—many of us could accept death without hesitation. It is harder to live for Him in the innumerable little refusals to follow selfish courses in which that life consists. So the Church, which is set in the world and has to carry on its activities through the instrumentality of worldly wealth, is under perpetual temptation to become attached to that wealth for its own sake; it is under obligation to resist that temptation; it does not follow that for the avoidance of the temptation it should abandon all wealth.

These are the considerations which constitute the inevitable interlocking of Church and State. Legal and constitutional arrangements make very little difference to it. There are features of the present "Establishment" in England which seem to me to be in the proper sense intolerable. The Church as a fellowship of worshippers ought to have absolute freedom to order its own worship without any restriction from persons and representatives of persons who may or may not be members of that fellowship. The subjection of the Church of England to Parliament in this respect is a prolific source of evils; but they are rather evils of lawlessness and insincerity than of undue servility to the State. What actually happens on a large scale is not that congregations find their mode of worship unduly controlled by the State, but that clergy square it with their consciences to break the law. This is a very great evil, but it is not precisely that evil which is often supposed to be inherent in the "Establishment."

It is not legal bonds that make the Church incline too closely to follow the State; it is personal ties and economic interests. We have spoken of the latter. They can be a source of deep spiritual corruption; and it is impossible for any man to know how seriously they bias his judgment through subconscious pressures. Yet even more serious, and entirely unavoidable, is the fact that the same persons are citizens of the State and members of the Church.

While the Church is very small, and especially if it is subject to persecution, it can stand apart from the life of society as a whole—a little spiritual fellowship bearing its witness by word and life, every member of it putting his Churchmanship before his citizenship. It hopes by degrees to absorb all citizens into itself, without loss of spiritual purity. But as it wins its way, and its roll of membership increases, persecution —perhaps after a temporary intensification—dies down. Children grow up in it who are schoolfellows of non-Christians, and are influenced alike by their Christian homes and by non-Christian companions; this involves some dilution. Persecution, which is good for the strengthening of faith and devotion but not good for the growth of charity, comes to an end. The Church becomes kindlier, but less intense. Citizens not wholly converted seek admission. The Church becomes fashionable. At last almost every one belongs to it, and it is now the religious aspect of a whole society of which the State is the civic aspect or function. How at this point is the Church to defy or oppose the State? Church and State are the same persons acting in different capacities.

This complete union of Church and State in the one Christian society was the medieval ideal. All were subject to both. But the mass of citizens took little part in the direction of either. The Church-function of the one society was exercised by "Churchmen"—that is, by the hierarchy; the State-function by the King and his Council. So the relations between Church and State expressed themselves in the struggles between Popes and Emperors, between a Thomas Becket and a Henry II.

68

Democracy and the spread of education have complicated rather than eased the problem. Nowadays every citizen takes a share in determining the policy of the State and every member of the Church takes a share in determining the action of the Church. When Churchmen and citizens are identical, it will follow that the Church is subservient to the State or exercises control over it in proportion as loyalty to Church or loyalty to State is the more prominent in the minds of the citizen-Churchmen.

So we come to the heart of the problem, which is not primarily organisation but a tension in the soul of the Christian citizen. He is a member of two societies; even if the membership of these two is identical, yet as societies they are two and not one. The distinctive functions of the two are governed by different principles, or rather by different relationships to one ultimate end—the glory of God in the welfare of His people.

Even if the citizens are all atheists, this is still the true goal of the State. It is sometimes proposed as a difference between Church and State that the Church is bound by allegiance to Jesus Christ and the State is not. But the State can only fulfil itself by conformity with the divine Logos, discharging those functions which are allotted to it by the Logos, which is the rational principle of the universe. And that Logos is known to Christians in Jesus Christ. But the State has its own method, which is appropriate for some purposes and not for all. This point has already been discussed (see pp. 36–7). Those who are

6

responsible for the administration of the State should recognise both the divine sanction of their office and the limitations of that office. If they are personally devoted Christians they are likely to do this; then the State will be efficient in its own department and will not invade that of the Church. If, however, these official persons have no religious faith, they will tend to draw all human activities within the sphere of the State, for it will be the most universal authority known to them.

Those who administer the affairs of the Church must in like manner recognise the divinely appointed sphere of the State and avoid invasion of this. But it is their function to remind Statesmen of their responsibility to God. "It is the duty of Lambeth to remind Westminster of its responsibility to God; but this does not mean that Westminster is responsible to Lambeth."

CHAPTER V

Churchman and Citizen

FROM all that has now been said it is evident that the problem of the relations between Church and State is primarily a problem in the mind and soul of each individual Christian. He is a member of the Church, because his faith in Christ unites him to all others who are upheld by that faith; and he is a citizen of his earthly State.

In his admirable study of *The Two Moralities*[1] the Master of Balliol presents with most delicate discriminations a parallel problem in terms of individual obligation and vocation. If readers of what I am now presenting will turn back to that admirable statement, it will in many ways elucidate the argument which I must now develop. But I am approaching the matter from a slightly different standpoint. The ordinary moral consideration of "my station and its duties" has its bearing upon my station as a member of the Church as well as upon my station as a member of the secular society; and the "morality of grace" makes its appeal to men who do not acknowledge the claim of Christ and in connexion with tasks commonly regarded as completely secular. Consequently the "two moralities" are not simply the morality of the citizen and the morality of the Churchman.

_____
[1] The first book of this series, published in 1940.

Citizen and Churchman alike are subject to both moralities.

There is here a manifest difference between the clergyman and the layman. The layman earns his living by an occupation which is also followed by men of other religious faiths or none. He seeks in his religion strength and inspiration to carry him through temptations, to help him to make his occupation a sphere of service rather than self-seeking, and to make him alert to opportunities of showing the spirit of Christ in dealing with his neighbours whether in the same occupation or outside it; but his work is "secular" in the sense that an unbeliever might do it, and many unbelievers actually do; it is a body waiting, so to speak, to be inspired. The clergyman earns his living by specifically religious activities. Religion is his business. This difference is very pervasive. There is here a great temptation for the clergyman. For all "business" is a concern with means rather than ends; but religion is concerned with the supreme end of man. The clergyman who, because religion is his business, treats religion as a business, has sold the pass; yet it is very easy to slip imperceptibly into doing this. Yet the clergyman needs to be "business-like"; and if he fails in this, he is likely to damage his purely religious work.

Thus even within the activity, and indeed within the very soul, of the group of persons who might seem wholly dedicated by their vocation to the cause of religion, the tension is to be found. It pervades all life for every Christian citizen. For the

72

non-Christian, of course, there is no such tension. Part of the lure of totalitarian doctrine and social order is that it eliminates this tension. If the State is made absolute and set in the place of God, there is no tension between God and the State. Nazi-ism thus provides a real solution at the cost of mutilating man's soul. Lutheranism had attempted a solution by allocating different spheres to Church and State. This inevitably results in pietism and the confinement of the Church to devotional exercises and hopes for a future life after death or a future world when this world has been broken up. Neither of these is compatible with the Christian conception of God as One God who is both Creator and Redeemer.

No; Church and State, religion and citizenship, have the same sphere—the life of man—but they have different functions in relation to that one sphere; and the Christian citizen has to fulfil his Churchmanship and his citizenship in the whole of his life by responding at all points to the appropriate claims of Church and State. We may set out a few of the contrasted yet related functions and then consider some of the practical bearings of these:

(1) The State stands for justice, the Church for love;

(2) For the State the material basis of life is primary; for the Church the spiritual source and goal of life is primary;

(3) The State is particular, the Church universal;

(4) The State is the organ of a natural community or of an association; the Church is called to be a

fellowship of the Spirit. (These terms will be interpreted when we discuss this contrast.)

(1) *The State stands for justice, the Church for love.*

We have already seen that the root of the principle of justice as we have come to understand it is man's relation to God. The Totalitarian States define justice as that treatment of the individual which most conduces to the welfare of the State. What the welfare of the State may be is not, so far as I know, anywhere defined. It would certainly include, and perhaps would chiefly consist in, the power of the State to maintain its will against other States and to impose its will upon them. But then we need to ask what its will is, and why it is this. When we press home the Totalitarian doctrines they are found to be in a high degree self-contradictory; and this is so because the essence of Totalitarianism is to treat as an end that which is essentially a means. The State is not an end in itself; it is a means to the good life of its citizens.

None the less it is very hard to resist the Totalitarian claim on any humanist basis; if a man has no status or worth except his status as a citizen and his worth to an earthly community, he can have no rights against the State which acts for that community. There can be no Rights of Man except on the basis of faith in God. But if God is real, and all men are His sons, that is the true worth of every one of them. My worth is what I am worth to God; and that is a marvellous great deal, for Christ died for me. Thus,

74

incidentally, what gives to each of us his highest worth gives the same worth to everyone; in all that matters most, we are all equal.

It is this dignity of man as one who has his own status among and even over against the whole multitude of his fellow citizens, and this equality in that supreme dignity, which provide the foundation of justice as western civilisation has learnt to understand it. What a man's rights should be in detail is a matter for the State to decide—as, for example, what are the rights of property-owners in respect of the property which they own? or what are the kinds of goods which may appropriately be private property? In the United States of America a national disaster occurred a few years ago through the ploughing up, for immediate financial gain, of acres of light soil, which afforded good but scanty pasture. The grass fibres had held the soil together. The breaking of these left it without cohesion, and in a season of gales following drought, it was so blown away that the land became useless as either arable or pasture. Yet there was strong feeling that it would be wrong, as interfering unduly with the liberty of the subject, to forbid by legislation the ploughing up of such land. Most of us in England regard such a feeling as completely unreasonable. The community should be able to prevent its own members from involving it in economic ruin for their own advantage. Yet the feeling in question, though misplaced, has roots in a most proper concern for the rights of the individual as against the tendency of the State to annihilate these in its concern for the general welfare. For what is that welfare except the securing of rights and interests of individuals in the most equitable manner? We condemn this feeling of resentment at restrictive legislation, not because the owner has no rights, but because other people have rights, and the coming generations have rights, and equity should be enforced among all of these. Justice is not primarily regard for the community as a whole; it is primarily regard for each and every individual concerned. The difference is not very great if we recognise that the community has no existence apart from its members, so that its welfare and theirs are identical. But even so there is a difference, and the right of appeal to the Crown acting judicially, against the Crown acting administratively, is a most sacred part of a civilised order. This should be abrogated or suspended only at moments when the interest of every citizen will be best served by the entrusting of unlimited power to the representatives of the whole community.

Justice is concerned with persons or parties having distinct interests which may come into conflict. It appears, therefore, to apply to a state of affairs where love is not yet supreme; and that is ultimately true; but it does not follow that love can, so to speak, leave justice behind. The Church, proclaiming the Gospel, calls all men to live by a perfect love which, if it universally prevailed, would supersede justice altogether. But this does not mean that if every individual were rooted and grounded in love, justice would thereupon be obsolete. The chief problems of

76

modern life concern the mutual relations of corporate groups—nations, employers' federations, trade unions, and the like. The predominance of love—of the desire to serve rather than to gain—in the hearts of the individuals concerned would vastly ease the task of settling the relations between the groups which they constitute and into which they are divided; but it would not of itself settle those relations.

At this point it would seem that the Church must give primary emphasis to the virtue which is the special concern of the State. Indeed I am convinced that one reason why the Church has counted for comparatively little in the public affairs of recent times is that its spokesmen have talked a great deal too much about love and not nearly enough about justice. Of course it is true that preachers of the Gospel cannot lay too great an emphasis on love as the supreme gift of God by receiving which man becomes for the first time capable of the good life which is God's design for him. But though a preacher cannot extol love too highly he may urge its claims irrelevantly. When he does this, the Christian who is a director of a railway company or the secretary of a trade union finds that what he has heard in sermons gives him no help with his problems. When a dispute arises concerning the proper rate of wages to be paid, the beautiful Christian relations between the two officials will facilitate friendly discussion and so increase the chance of a reasonable settlement; but they will not actually produce that settlement. If all the shareholders and all the wage-earners were inspired

77

by the same lofty sentiments, no doubt a settlement
fair to both sides would always be reached. But that
is not the fact; for many years to come it will not be
the fact; it is a probable hypothesis that on this planet
it will never be the fact. But if shareholders care more
about their own dividends than about the comfort of
the wage-earners, it being presumed that no question
of serious distress is involved, and if the wage-earners
care more for their own families' comfort than for
increased ease among shareholders, the director and
the secretary are bound, not only by the terms of
their employment but by moral obligation, to do the
best they can for their own clients; and the fact that
each loves the other as himself, if it is a fact, will only
ease the discussion, not provide the solution.

What was the duty of Admiral Sommerville before
Oran in July 1940? He was, of course, to do what
best served the cause of love, but not what love of
the French Admiral might suggest. His duty was to
destroy those French ships which might otherwise
have fallen into German hands and be used to extend
the Nazi tyranny. But a sermon about love would
probably not have directly prompted this.

Is it not the fact that in problems concerning the
relations of corporate groups of men, the way of love
lies through justice? We cannot leave the influence
of the Gospel without effect upon this vast area of
human experience until approximately all men are
devout Christians whose lives express their faith. We
say that Christianity can solve the problems of the
world; and men of the world wrestling with those

problems answer: "Then for God's sake show us how." The reply must be twofold: (i) When all men perfectly respond to the Gospel the problems will be so transformed as to be fairly described as done away; (ii) in the meantime, let that love which fills the heart of the true worshipper become an added impulse to the search for justice.

Indeed in the relations which we are chiefly considering justice is the proper expression of love. If two nations with conflicting interests, or two parties to an industrial dispute, will state their case as forcibly as they can before the most impartial tribunal available, with full intention of accepting the award, each is recognising the other as standing on a level with itself and that is the first step in obedience to the second of the two great commandments.

What the Christian citizen has to do in most of his problems is to dedicate himself in the power of love to the establishment of justice. That is the way in which his Churchmanship and his citizenship may converge upon a line of Christian civic or economic action.

Of course perfect justice will not be reached; so long as it is envisaged as the proper balance between conflicting selfish interests it will scarcely ever be found; perfect justice is a product of perfect love, not a stage on the way to it. None the less we know roughly what justice is; it is that balance between claims which a fair-minded man strikes after reviewing all the relevant factors in the situation. There is no general principle which determines in advance the

79

just allocation of profits as between dividends and wages. At a time of national need there is a call for equality of sacrifice, but this does not mean that all give to the State an identical amount (for then the poor would be ruined before the rich felt the difference) or even a numerically proportionate amount (for a rich man may give ten per cent without altering his way of life, while a poor man must change his personal habits if he gives two per cent). Equality of sacrifice can only mean that everyone contributes in such a way as to be similarly affected. It is a general standard of reference, not a measuring-stick.

Yet to a remarkable degree men of goodwill can usually be brought to substantial agreement about what justice requires in a given instance. That is why men who differ widely about the goal to be aimed at commonly agree, if brought together, about the next step to be taken; and as that is the only step that can be taken at all, this is the only agreement that is practically important. The upshot for the Christian citizen is clear; while the Church exists to preach love, and the State to maintain justice, the Christian citizen draws on the inspiration of love to establish a closer approximation to real justice. We shall see some of the implications of this shortly.

(2) *For the State the material basis of life is primary; for the Church the spiritual source and goal of life is primary.*

The attempt to allot the material to the State and the spiritual to the Church is alluring but quickly found to be futile. For the State must have some principles to guide its control of material wealth, and the Church as an organisation at work in the world inevitably becomes an agent in the economic sphere. In the modern world this is perhaps the most important point in the interaction of Church and State. There are extreme limits at which the functions of either stretch beyond the concern of the other. The State which came into being, as Aristotle observed, "for the sake of life" is concerned with actually providing the physical basis of life as the Church is not. Yet even here the Church comes in, for neglect or mismanagement of this function by the State may lead to great suffering and bitterness of spirit. The Church is fully entitled to say to the State, "You must not let men starve."

At the other end there is the eternal destiny of man with which the State is not directly concerned; but if man is indeed destined for eternal life in fellowship with God, that is a fact so important in his whole nature that the State must take note of it, and have a care that the facts of life which fall under its own control are not so ordered as to hinder the citizens from qualifying for their eternal destiny.

Between these two limits there is opportunity for limitless interplay. In former times the Church was the main agency for the relief of the poor. The Monasteries did much of the work of the modern Relieving Officer; and it was partly because the Monasteries had been dissolved that the State found itself obliged to pass the first English Poor Law at the end of the reign of Queen Elizabeth. Till very recent times the Poor Fund was a real factor in the social life of most villages and of many urban parishes. Here the Church was dealing with individual needs. Since the State, nationally or locally, has undertaken the administration of relief by an elaborate and complicated system the part of the Church is changed. It cannot properly advocate in its own name methods of improving that system, for these involve judgments of expediency as well as of principle. Its part is two-fold. It must keep alive in men's minds the contrast that exists between any earthly ordering of society and any that would correspond to the standard of Christ; in the England of our time it must point to permanent facts with which the Christian conscience cannot be content. For example, many people are still living in conditions which give wholly inadequate opportunities for family life, and even for elementary decencies; children suffer from malnutrition; and the industrial life of the country is disgraced by chronic unemployment. The Church is both entitled and obliged to condemn the society characterised by these evils; but it is not entitled in its corporate capacity to advocate specific remedies.

On the other hand, the very object of condemning the evil is to stimulate those who respect its authority to seek and to apply the remedy. Far the larger proportion of the Church's contribution to social progress is made in this way. It inspires its members with a faith in the power of which they, acting as politicians, civil servants, business men, trade unionists, or whatever they may be, modify the customs and traditions of the department of state or section of society with which they are concerned.

In other words the Church lays down principles; the Christian citizen applies them; and to do this he utilizes the machinery of the State.

If, as seems certain, the end of the war is bound to usher in a vast social transformation, the Church must be ready with its system of principles, and the Christian citizens must be ready to press for attention to these in the action taken by the State. It would be out of place to attempt to set out the system of principles here; but in order to illustrate the point which is being pressed, it may be well to sketch a Christian analysis of the situation in some of its aspects. There will be in this nothing distinctively Christian, in the sense of being directly deducible from the Gospel or incapable of apprehension apart from the Gospel; it results from a consideration of the "natural order," by which is meant the consideration of the various departments of life in the light of the essential function of each. But for a Christian this "natural order" or "natural law" is God's order, God's law. It is our duty to God both to find it and to act upon it.

In this order it is evident that the object or end of production is consumption. Corn is grown that the people may eat bread. If then in a world where some people are hungry food is destroyed because there is no "market" for it, something has gone wrong. It seems that the producer is not growing the corn in order to feed the people, which is the object of corn-growing in the natural order, but in order to make a profit for himself. The result of trusting to the profit-motive has been the strange phenomenon of "poverty in the midst of plenty"; and the only solution proposed by those who rely on the profit-motive is to abolish the plenty! During the nineteenth century the essentially false basis of our economic structure was concealed by the apparently limitless expansion of markets. Search for profits led to increased production; and this always found a market somewhere. But that process has come to an end. Because the market is now limited, it becomes the arena of fierce competition. Tariff walls are erected by each nation in the hope of securing some market relatively free from alien intrusion. The whole system of mutual supply is converted into one of internecine rivalries of which war is the logical outcome.

But we ought never to have started down that road; and we must now, however painfully, retrace our steps. We must begin to organise our industry with the supply of need as the primary aim and the making of profits as entirely incidental. This is a return to the "natural order" as it exists in the mind of the Creator; but of course it is a reversal of the order natural to the selfishness of men! The Church cannot say how it is to be done; but it is called to say that it must be done, and to demand of those upon whom the change will impose sacrifices that

84

they accept these with goodwill in the name of fellowship and service.

There the Church stops, and the State, moved by its citizens and by the Christian impulse communicated through them from the Church, takes up the task. There is room here for abundance of divergent opinions. Shall the method be Communal Ownership? or Limitation of Profits through a statutory scheme? or control by the workers, managerial and manual, who will hire capital as they need it instead of being themselves hired by the owners of capital? There are many ways in which the essential business—the elimination of the search for profits as a primary factor—might be brought about. If the citizens examine these in a Christian spirit with a Christian purpose, it is likely that the State will find a course sufficient in practical wisdom to secure the benefit aimed at while avoiding disaster on the way. But this will only happen if the Church is proclaiming the principles, and the citizen is conscious of his Churchmanship. The latter requirement becomes even more important in connexion with what follows.

(3) *The State is particular, the Church universal.*

All secular organisations are particular; some day there may be "The Parliament of Man, the Federation of the World"; but too plainly that day is very far off. A man is a member of his family, of his school and college, his trade union or professional society, his nation. Every one of these makes claims upon him; to each he owes a loyalty. The extent to which these loyalties affect a man's sense of duty is astonishing to all those who have not carefully observed and reflected on it. A man who is tender-hearted in all his personal dealings will give his vote on a board of directors without a qualm in support of a policy involving ruin to many—as, for example, the installation of labour-saving machinery, which leaves on the scrap-heap the labourers who are "saved." It may be right to do this; but it ought to be appreciated as presenting an ethical problem. No statesman, it may be presumed, declares war with such indifference to the human suffering involved. But the problem which here reaches its acutest phase is pervasive of that whole area of life where men act for collective units rather than in their own names.

We have already spoken of the relation of justice to love in these connexions. What falls here to be observed is that there is no hope that either side to a dispute will truly aim at justice unless there is an over-arching loyalty which checks, and sets in its right perspective, the sectional loyalty which each party feels so strongly. In cases where the interests at stake are less than the greatest, respect for a recognised code of conduct may meet the need; this is in reality a loyalty to common humanity. But where the interests touched are felt to be vital, this restraint is likely to be ineffective. The driving force of a sectional loyalty, calling as it does on the altruistic and egoistic impulses alike, is very great. It will not be held in check except by a loyalty equally strong to a fellowship of which members of the opposing party are members.

The Church, as we saw, is in its aim such an all-inclusive fellowship, the proper object of such an over-arching loyalty. If St. Paul's apprehension of it were fully verified we should expect to see the Christians on both sides of an industrial dispute get together and work out a fair adjustment for which they would then stand in their several camps. Similarly we should expect to see the Christians on both sides of an international dispute establish contact with a view to framing a policy which would be just to both sides, or (for they might well lack the specialist knowledge for that task) with a view to generating an atmosphere conducive to methods of conciliation. What is known as the Ecumenical Movement represents a movement of the spirit in the hearts of Christian people towards this goal.

The Church as historically organised has seldom fulfilled this role. There are two main reasons for this. One is to be found in its own divisions. How can a disunited Church call rival parties or nations to the way of agreement? One reason for pressing forward the work of Christian reunion is that there are essential functions of the Church for which a divided Church is disqualified. But more is needed than reunion in Faith and Order. Roman Catholics have fought each other in national wars despite their unity in Church-membership. What is needed is that the citizen should be conscious of his Churchmanship in his civic activities. This is indeed at all times the real practice of our religion—that we think of our various activities and the people we have to do with, and also of our Lord at the same time. We need to see how our business enterprises, our patriotic service, our human relationships, look in the light of that Presence. So in every form of rivalry or of potential or actual hostility, the Christian citizen should be conscious of his unity in Christ with his fellow Christians on the other side. Often this might turn hostility into co-operation; always it would secure that the hostility, if such there must be, is of action only, never of the heart, and will so prepare the way for reconciliation and restored fellowship.

The Churchman in his distinctively religious acts can serve the Church Universal—by his share in its worship, by his prayers, by his support of its work of proclaiming the Gospel to every creature. The Christian citizen cannot directly serve any universal society. He must act where he is in the groups to which he belongs. His method must not be to eliminate the narrower loyalties, for that will only leave him a bewildered atom in a world too vast for him to affect. But he must use each wider loyalty to check his fulfilment of the narrower. He must not so serve his family or class as to injure his nation; he must not so serve his nation as to injure mankind. This course he will be enabled to follow if he can become deeply and continuously conscious of his membership in and loyalty to the one fellowship which even aspires to be all-embracing, the Universal Church.

(4) *The State is the organ of a natural community or of an association; the Church is called to be a fellowship of the Spirit.*

It is not commonly recognised that there are many distinct ways in which human beings are brought together in collective units, and that the psychology and in some respects the ethics of those units vary accordingly. There are at least three quite distinct types. I think the others are variations or combinations of these. But the three which we shall consider are certainly distinct. Every Christian citizen belongs to two, and nearly every one to all the three. First, there is the Natural Community, of which the family is the most evident type; a true "nation" is also a natural community. The chief characteristics of such a community are that men are born into it and therefore belong to it apart from any act of choice. It is a given fact, and as such it is its own end. Religious people will claim—truly—that its end is the glory of God. But it exists apart from any recognition of that; and normally it subserves the glory of God by being its own true self. Certainly the conception of itself held by its members will differ according as they do or do not believe in God. To that we shall return. At present we note that the end of a natural community is to be itself, and that it subserves the glory of God by being what He created it to be.

Secondly, there is the Association, a collective unit constituted by the deliberate choice of its members for the promotion of some object, commercial, cultural, or of some other kind. The members may be brought into personal intimacy or they may have no dealings with one another apart from the forwarding of the object of the Association. This will depend on the level of human interest at which the Association operates, as will more fully appear in the discussion.

Thirdly, there is the true Fellowship; as the Greek word translated "fellowship" in English clearly implies, this is a partnership in something else. The "fellowship of the Holy Spirit" does not mean the companionship of the Holy Spirit, though without this it could not exist. It means a union of all Christians in the fact that the Holy Spirit is with and within them. A true fellowship is not created by the choice of its members. Nor does it, like a natural community, exist apart from any choice of its members. But the members are brought into it by a power—of the Spirit or of some ideal due to His inspiration—which works upon and through their will and choice. It is not apart from my will that I am a Christian, for I can choose to repudiate Christianity and become an apostate; but neither is it due to my will. The Holy Spirit, acting through parents and teachers, has made me a Christian, claiming my devotion so that I cannot without conscious guilt refuse it.

Every Christian is a member of the natural community which is his family and of the natural community which is his nation. He is also a member of the Church which is called to be a true Fellowship. Besides these he is in fact likely to be a member of several Associations.

If he is to fulfil his function in these various

90

memberships he must both attend to the nature of the collective units to which he belongs so as to act in proper harmony with this, and must also consider the relation of these types of grouping to one another.

(1) The Natural Community, because it is essentially its own end, has an initial egoism which is part of its very being. It exists to be itself. If it goes out of existence, one constituent of the scheme of things is lost. It is a sense of this, sometimes coupled with a belief in the purpose of God in creation, which leads to a sense of obligation to defend such a community by all possible means and at any sacrifice. The family is, in a civilised country, hardly ever the object of direct attack, so the occasion does not arise; but at a primitive stage of civilisation where family rivalries lead to direct personal strife, the family is found to call forth a loyalty expressed in the very ways in which national loyalty is expressed among us.

If a man tries to break away from these native loyalties he is far more likely to sink than to rise in the moral scale. He must accept the given facts concerning himself and work forward from there; and among those given facts are his membership of his family and nation. If he is to serve mankind he must do it by serving them, using the wider loyalty, as was said, to check excesses which the narrower might prompt.

The Christian citizen does not attempt to escape from his citizenship; but he interprets it in the light of his Christian faith. He regards his family and nation as there, and as being what they are, by the action of God's providence, except so far as they have spoilt the divine intention by their own self-will. If he stops here, he may become a kind of Nazi, believing that God has called his own nation to dominate others. But if his faith in God is really Christian he cannot so interpret any part of the divine purpose. The God whose Majesty is specially revealed in the act of the Lord washing His disciples' feet, will not call His strong nations to lord it over the rest of His family. There may be need, even a divine call, to stand by force for righteousness against an unrighteous abuse of force; but the notion of an essentially conquering mission is incompatible with the character of God revealed in Christ.

The Christian citizen, then, will be a genuine patriot as part of His response to what God has done for him; but he will never be a "Jingo." He will serve his country in arms or in peaceful ways, taking as the guide of his service all in his country's tradition which is most akin to the Spirit of Christ. A British citizen will not be less glad of the British Empire because of his Christianity; but this will make him careful to attach his joy to its record of justice, freedom, and trustworthiness, not to its mere extent or the capacity of British people to impose their will on others. And proportionate to his joy in all that is admirable in the record will be his shame and penitence for whatever in it is base or greedy or cruel. Few things are so important for the shaping of imperial policy in the long run as the grounds of the delight which citizens take in the history of country and empire.

If this is grounded in the noblest elements it will lead us to develop these and to check whatever tendencies may appear which are contrary to these.

(2) In addition to his membership in family and nation, almost everyone is a member of various associations. Sometimes this arises from his occupation by which he earns his livelihood, as in the case of a managing director of a company. Anyhow, the claim of his employment has always to be met, and it will often give him opportunity to influence some department of life in a Christian direction. But we are at the moment specially concerned with the various particular loyalties which arise from the groupings in which men find themselves through their professional or personal interests. Where an association is concerned with the means of life, as every commercial enterprise is, it is a weak bond of union. Men may be associated in a scheme for "developing" some remote part of the earth without thereby forming any personal attachments; it may even be that each is interested in nothing except his own share of the proceeds. If, as often happens, a friendship results from meeting over business, this is independent of the association and its purposes. Such an association has its own aim, and as this may easily bring it into rivalry with others, it tends to develop a certain sort of egoism. But this is not like the egoism of a nation, where the interest of the community outstrips and may overwhelm that of the individual; in this case the egoism of the association is merely the combined egoisms of its members. Each wants all

93

he can get, so together they seek the largest possible gains.

Yet the sense of acting as a body has even here a soporific effect upon conscience. Though each is really seeking his own interest through the combined effort, he conceals this from himself by reflection that he is acting for the common interest of all the associates, and thereby excludes from the arena of his concern all other, perhaps conflicting, interests. Appalling cruelties have before now been perpetrated by men individually gentle, when banded together for some wealth-making project.

Here the Christian should be able to call to his aid the memory that all men are children of his heavenly Father whose love goes out to them all. This will check any excesses due to the corporate egoism of the association, without interfering with the loyalty proper among partners in any undertaking.

A trade union begins as an association, but grows to be something akin to a natural community. The ablest boys born to wage-earning parents can by scholarships make their way into the salaried occupations. But those who remain in the wage-earning class were born in it and grew up in it. That class, with its distinctive institutions, becomes a real community for them, with the same appeal to their devotion and the same natural corporate egoism. The propertied class is less self-conscious, as is to be expected, until its status is attacked. Then it reveals itself also as, at least for defensive purposes, a community very tenacious of its standing. It has been rather startling in these last years to see how accurately the political Right in all countries has verified the predictions of Karl Marx and shown a tendency to let class-interests and class-sympathies prevail over considerations more important to the national community. That the Left should be Marxian consciously or unconsciously was to be expected; but it is arguable that the Right has in fact corresponded the more closely to the pattern drawn for it by Marx. Anyhow, the point is that an association founded on the self-interest of its members may easily develop the qualities, especially the less admirable qualities, of a natural community.

But an association may also develop some of the qualities of a true fellowship. Many a trade union has done this, through the closeness of the intercourse of its members and concern for the more ideal elements in its aims. Still more evident is this process in associations formed directly for cultural or ideal aims. In such cases the bond of union is a truly personal concern in the members. I recall how marked this characteristic was in the early years of the Workers Educational Association. This aimed at increasing educational opportunities for working-class folk; therein it had an aim beyond itself. It was an almost purely altruistic aim, and it was pursued with missionary zeal. In fact there was more of evangelistic quality about those early W.E.A. gatherings than about most assemblies convened under any such name or description. But over and above this was the genuine fellowship of the members. The cause that brought them together was not concerned with the means of life, as in a commercial enterprise, but with the very quality of life. Consequently it was able to effect a truly personal union.

The way in which egoism tends to pervert an association is through eagerness for credit or anxiety about prestige. It is concerned to promote some good cause; it is natural that the members should be glad for it to have the credit for any advance gained. But this must never be allowed to interfere with the cause itself. An illustration is afforded by an episode in the history of the W.E.A. In its work of increasing educational facilities for working-class people, it had been successful in establishing Joint Committees in all the Universities, consisting in equal numbers of University representatives chosen by the University and representatives of Labour chosen by or through the W.E.A. These Joint Committees established and supervised Tutorial Classes in working-class districts. Then some trade unions approached the Universities direct, and the Universities were ready to supply their demand. But one or two local branches of the W.E.A. tried to resist this, insisting that all applications to the University must be dealt with by the Joint Committee. There was probably some administrative convenience in this; but it was raised as a point of principle. Very few branches took this jealous line and the association as a whole gave them no support. Evidently, if more educational work could be done that way, the new move was to be welcomed, even though it broke down what had been a practical monopoly of the W.E.A.

The Christian citizen who is a member or officer of any association must work loyally with the association. He is not at liberty to think out for himself what is on Christian grounds the best course of action and then take that course. He may commend it to his fellow members; and if he persuades them he and they will follow it together. But he is bound to act with the association or withdraw from it. On the other hand he may be able to do much, while remaining in it and co-operating in actions which seem to him other than the best, to bring it nearer to a Christian standard than it would be without his effort.

A great difficulty may often be experienced by the conscientious member of any group with regard to the point at which he ought to withdraw from co-operation. Lord Palmerston is reported to have kept a special drawer for Mr. Gladstone's resignations, and the problem of a Cabinet Minister is a very clear example of what we are considering. He presumably holds that it is good for the country that his party should remain in power; he has reason to suppose that his resignation would weaken its authority and might lead to a change of Government; on one important issue he disagrees with or even disapproves the action to which his colleagues, and he with them, are committed. Evidently there is no hard and fast rule by which such a situation can be resolved. He has to strike a balance as fairly as he can, remembering that in such a matter his personal relations with his colleagues ought not to count for more than a trifle,

97

and that he must judge the advantages and disadvantages of either course by a Christian standard of value.

(3) Over against the natural community and the association with their different types of egoism stands the genuine Fellowship, the Fellowship of the Spirit, in which, so far as it is true to its own nature, there is no place for any egoism. Some associations approximate to this, but to be such a fellowship is the essential vocation of the Church and of the Church alone.

In some respects this Fellowship reproduces the characteristics of both the natural community and of the association; for it is its own end, and to be fully and completely itself is the whole of its vocation; yet also it exists to promote certain ends, the conversion of the heathen world and the conforming of the life of the converted world to the standards of the Gospel.

It is its own end. It is part of its own creed. It exists to be itself. The life of Heaven is the life of the perfected Church—the perfect Fellowship of finite spirits indwelt by the Holy Spirit. So long as any race remains outside this Fellowship, the Fellowship itself is defective and the Body of Christ lacks one of its limbs or members. Thus in converting the world the Church is completing or perfecting itself, extensively, and in conforming the converted world, which is itself, to the standards of the Gospel it is completing or perfecting itself intensively.

But the primary characteristic of the Church is neither its missionary enterprise which is the essence of Apostolicity, nor its universal scope which is its Catholicity, but the fact that it is constituted by the redeeming act of God in Christ and is sustained by the indwelling divine Spirit, or in short its Holiness. And the first way in which it is called to be itself is neither through missionary extension nor through influence upon national life but through inward sanctification. Its essential quality is to be a Fellowship of persons so fully possessed by the Spirit of Christ that for practical purposes they are limbs of His body and there is only one person there—Christ Himself. All divisions among men, whether due to religious history, or to culture, or to economic status, are to be negligible; there is to be "one man in Christ Jesus." So St. Paul apprehended the true reality of the Church, which entitles it to be called the Church.

The actual society of Christians does not present that appearance and has never done so. St. Paul had to deal with episodes within its life as remote as possible from that ideal. And the reason is, of course, the incompleteness of the conversion, dedication, sanctification of its several members.

As a result of this the Church loses the distinctive quality of true Fellowship—a union of all through the control of each by one Spirit—and becomes an Association, a voluntary organisation of persons concerned to provide satisfaction for their religious appetites and those of others. As such an association the State inevitably regards it. For the State all groupings are compulsory or voluntary; and on that basis of division, the Church is voluntary. The pity is that it so largely lives and works at that level. Then it becomes as self-defensive as any other human association. It interprets the confiscation of its property as an attack upon itself, and tries, as medieval Popes habitually tried, to throw the protection of the sanctity to which it is called over the property which it has acquired. The Church, as Church, has no interest in establishment, endowment, or any such thing. Its officers and members are very much interested in these matters as Christian citizens or even as personally affected, but not as members of the Body of Christ who had not where to lay His head.

This detachment to which the Church is called, but which Churchmen have seldom attained, is not a hermit-like withdrawal from the world; on the contrary it is the way by which the Church may most influence the world. For the way to spiritual power over the world lies through worship and sanctification. If the Church is to supply to Christian people the quality enabling them to convert the world, they (or at least a large proportion of them) must be Churchmen before they are citizens, recognising that their highest duty and privilege is to worship God made known in Jesus Christ, to quicken their consciences by His holiness, to feed their minds on His truth, to purify their imaginations by His beauty, to open their hearts to His love, to submit their wills to His purpose. Worship includes all those elements. Worship so understood is the activity whereby and wherein men become more fully incorporated into the Body of

Christ, thus enabling the Church to become its true self and to do its true work.

Of course such worship is a continuous and life-long enterprise. To "go to Church" and there sit, stand, and kneel while other people say things and sing things may be better than nothing, for it is an act of witness; but it is not certain that it is better than nothing, for such a Churchgoer lowers the temperature of the whole congregation. It is not possible to worship truly while the daily life is far from God; and it is not possible to bring the daily life much nearer to God except by the best worship of which we are capable.

Thus worship is the distinctive and specially characteristic activity of the Church; but then worship includes all life and the moments spent in concentrated worship, whether "in Church" or elsewhere, are the focussing points of the sustaining and directing energy of the worshipper's whole life.

It would strike many people as absurd to say that the cure for unemployment it to be found through worship; but it would be quite true.

If then the Christian citizen is to make his Christianity tell upon his politics, his business, his social enterprises, he must be a Churchman—consciously belonging to the worshipping fellowship and sharing its worship—before he is a citizen; he must bring the concerns of his citizenship and his business before God, and go forth to them carrying God's inspiration with him.

This is all expressed in the Eucharist. There we

bring familiar forms of economic wealth, which is always the product of man's labour exercised upon God's gifts, and offer them as symbols of our earthly life. If God had not given to the seed its life and to the soil the quality to nurture it, there would be neither harvest nor bread. Equally, if man had not ploughed the soil and scattered the seed, there would be neither harvest nor bread. Bread is a product of man's labour exercised upon God's gift for the satisfaction of man's need. So is wine. These are our "oblations" at the "offertory"—often also accompanied by "alms" expressing the charity which seeks to share with others the good things which God has given to us.

These representatives of all earthly "goods" we offer to God in union with the act of Christ at the Last Supper when, in preparatory interpretation of His death, He took the bread, called it His Body, and broke it—took the wine, called it His Blood and gave it. Because we have offered our "earthly" goods to God, He gives them back to us as heavenly goods, binding us into union with Christ in that self-offering which is His royalty, so that we give not only our goods but ourselves, and thus become strengthened as members of His Body to do His will in the various departments of our life.

The Eucharist divorced from life loses reality; life devoid of worship loses direction and power. It is the worshipping life that can transform the world.

History is full of illustrations of this truth. But it is also, even more continuously, full of the opportunities which were lost because the actual Church was not a true Church, not a Body of Christ responsive in all its members to His Spirit.

If the Church is not like that the fault is in the members, who are so imperfectly subordinated to the Head. If the Church in my country, in my parish, is not like that, it is partly because my own response to Christ and my own self-dedication are so incomplete.

When Christians in sufficient numbers are truly converted, dedicated, sanctified, they will make the several associations which they serve handmaids of the one Divine Family, and they will make their natural communities provinces in the Kingdom of God. The Christian has no need to be greatly interested in the question how far this may come to pass on earth. That it should come to pass must be our prayer and effort. But history in any case derives its meaning from a consummation beyond itself, and what is begun here may be perfected hereafter.

QUESTIONS FOR GROUP STUDY

CHAPTER I

What light is thrown on the problem of Church and State by the Scottish Disruption of 1843 which resulted in the formation of the "Church of Scotland Free," by the nineteenth-century agitations for disestablishment, particularly the disestablishment of the Church of Ireland, and by the House of Lords decision in the United Free Church case? (p. 1).

What should be the relation of theology to history, economics, political theory, natural science? (p. 2).

In what sense can it be said that Christianity claims to base its belief and practice upon a divine Revelation? Describe revelation in this connexion (p. 3).

Illustrate the statement that each of the sections into which Christendom split at the Reformation claims the authority which could only belong to the united body, none succeeding in exercising it (p. 5).

"The only way for the Church to escape the authority of the State is to own no property at all; and that would be a deprivation of means to do spiritual work such as it would be madness to incur unless the alternative were a compromise of fundamental principles." Is it possible for a religious society to "own no property at all" if it is anything more than a tiny group living in one place? What conditions would make holding property a compromise of fundamental principles? (p. 12).

APPENDIX TO CHAPTER I

What are the implications of the view that man's spirit cannot rightly be coerced? (p. 17).

CHAPTER II

Would you say that the Social Contract theories of the State are a modern expression of the earlier theological doctrine that the State is a result of the Fall, while St. Paul's admiration of the State and the Anglican theory of non-resistance are the basis of the Conservative theory which makes the unity of the State logically prior to the freedom of individuals and groups within it? (p. 23).

What aspects of social life are appropriately controlled by universal rules? (p. 25).

Is the individual ever justified in using force? Are any groups within the State ever justified in using force? In answering these questions, make clear the content of the word "force"; does it include economic as well as physical force? (p. 25).

"The state is essentially the source of law" (p. 26). What happens if the State makes unjust laws? Can the State break the law it has made? Who is to define justice? Can the individual appeal from the law of Britain to the law of God?

The Archbishop defines the limitations of the rightful authority of the State, positively by saying that all that is purely temporal in the citizen is rightly subject to it, negatively by saying that it may not claim the subservience of his conscience and that his spiritual integrity and his fellowship with God take precedence of his citizenship (p. 29). Is the State justified, then, in censoring books, pictures, and plays, and if so, on what grounds? The judgment that a work of art is indecent is partly an expression of aesthetic convention and of non-rational inhibitions. Is the policeman or magistrate competent and has the State the right to destroy books and pictures on the ground that they are indecent? If conscience is exempt from State control, can books and newspapers be suppressed on the ground that they are immoral; that they attack the received standards of conduct? Has the State the right to silence men whose writings are

blasphemous? If so, why? May the State decree that
Darwinism may not be taught in science laboratories
subsidised by public money? May it forbid its pro-
fessors of economics to teach Communism? Is it justified
in punishing men for teaching that all participation in war
is sinful?

Has there ever been a state which has been the organ of
the community, rather than of one group of citizens, and
has existed to serve the citizens, and not one class? Would
the English proletariat be justified in rebelling to throw out
of the seat of power the present class tyranny? (pp. 29, 30).

Justify and illustrate the three statements contained in:
"Not every sinful action is a crime, nor is it desirable to
make it so; but in a well-ordered state every crime is also
a sin." If possible, illustrate the implied statement that that
state is not well ordered in which there are crimes which
are not sins (p. 30).

"The State, as organ of the community, may rightly be
concerned with all that takes place in the life of the community." Criticise this. Does it get its plausibility from
the vagueness of its verb—"be concerned with"? (p. 33).

"The State is an instrument of God for the preservation
of justice and for the promotion of human welfare so far
as this can be done by universal enactment or through
opportunities created by universal enactment." Give illustrations to show what is included and what is excluded by
this definition (p. 36).

CHAPTER III

A sacrament degenerates into magic if a material form
or vehicle designed by spirit for its own self-expression
survives when there is no spiritual purpose or meaning
which uses it for self-expression. Can you give examples
of this from the past and present practice of Christians,
within as well as beyond the borders of your own section
of the Christian Church? (p. 42).

Is it relevant to mention the resurrection of the body in discussing the relation of the spiritual to the physical? If so, how do you define "body" and "physical"? (p. 42).

What is the relation of the Church which is the Body of Christ and, as some hold, the Kingdom of God to the actual phenomenal society: in parishes, the vicar and church-wardens and the members of the Parochial Church Council —human, all too human; in rural deaneries, the clergy who would be so ordinary if vanity did not lead to so many eccentricities; in diocesan conferences, which are not quite sure whether the man who pays the piper should call the tune, or the man who has the unction of God's grace; in the National Assembly, where so many are concerned with the stipends of the clergy, the rights of patrons, and whether Churchmen should be required to bow to the altar in their cathedral church? (p. 44).

In the light of the divisions of Christendom, and of the fact that all churches have erred "not only in their living and manner of ceremonies, but also in matters of Faith," what do we mean when we say that we believe in One Holy Catholic Church?

"It can hardly be said that the Church ought to denounce the State every time the State acts on less than absolutely Christian principles." Do you agree with this, or would you say that it is the duty and privilege of the Church always to challenge the relativities of actual politics with the Absolute of the will of God? (p. 51).

What are the non-Christian pressures which tend to keep the Bishops silent when the government of a democratic country takes action which is less than Christian? (p. 52).

Give examples from the last fifty years of occasions when the clergy, or any considerable section of them, supported policies on moral grounds which were also financially advantageous to themselves or to the Church. Do the clergy identify their own interests and prestige with the triumph of the Kingdom of God? (p. 53).

Discuss the view that disestablishment is, properly speaking, of no interest to the Church (p. 54).

Examine the relevant Biblical material and, in the light of it, discuss the four doctrines outlined in this chapter of the relation of the Church to the Kingdom of God (p. 55).

CHAPTER IV

It is not the function of the clergy to formulate political and economic policies (even when they are secretaries of the Industrial Christian Fellowship or the Christian Social Council) but to stimulate the laity and remind them of the principles which are the relevant corollaries of the Christian Faith. Examine this distinction between policy and principle. Do they meet or overlap anywhere? In the next chapter a distinction is drawn between expediency, left to the State, and principle, rightly judged by the Church. Is this the same distinction? (p. 61).

May we take the Archbishop's principle a step farther and say: if to insist on some point of doctrine would involve the forfeiture of property held as a means of ministering to the rich, it is evident that a balance of advantage and disadvantage must be struck? (p. 63).

"Prudence is a virtue and fanaticism is not." Discuss this by illustrating and defining the terms used (p. 64).

Do you agree that with the Cross and Resurrection His Kingdom came with power? (p. 65).

"While the Church is very small" (p. 67). How far is it true that the marks of the Church in Ephesians in particular and in the New Testament in general are only possible so long as the Church is a small group? It has been said that much of the talk about "Christian fellowship" is literally thoughtless in the conditions of large urban congregations and enormous parishes.

CHAPTER V

In what way does the behaviour which expresses love differ from that which expresses justice? "Love your enemies." Is there any specifically Christian behaviour, (a) of a British soldier towards a German soldier; (b) of a British civilian towards a civilian enemy alien; (c) to "Germany" or to Germans in general? (p. 73).

"We must begin to organise our industry with the supply of need as the primary aim and the making of profits as entirely incidental." Does this mean that we *count on* Christian, i.e. converted shareholders, directors, workpeople? Or is it enough to expect enlightened self-interest? (p. 84).

What has been done, and what can be done, by English Christians to maintain spiritual fellowship in these days of war with German and Italian Christians? (p. 87).

What are you doing to bring about the reunion of Christendom? Are your prayers for that object anything more than words? What thoughts go with the words? And what deeds? (p. 87).

In what ways does your Churchmanship make you conscious that the Church is, at least in idea, all-embracing and universal? In what ways, as you examine it, do you realise that you have fallen short in this? Can you suggest methods by which the catholicity of the Church might be brought home to the consciousness of Anglicans? (p. 88).

Is the Catholic Church the only example of a true Fellowship, a truly personal community? Can you suggest any others? (p. 90).

The family in England has been accused of becoming a tyranny and an offence (see Mr. Bernard Shaw's prefaces, especially that to *Getting Married*). Patriotism is said by some to be one of the greatest curses that afflict the modern world. Would it not be better to brush aside these lesser loyalties and seek to express one's share in the Mind of the

Race by working to set up a World State and to make effective one's membership in it? (pp. 91, 92).

Where do the clergy belong in the Marxian picture? With the wage-earners or with the propertied class? Many clergy will claim to belong with neither, but what is the truth? (p. 95).

There is no place for any egoism in the Church so far as it is true to its own nature. After all, who cares what happens to the Church of England if only the Kingdom of our Lord Jesus Christ is exalted and extended? What criticism do you offer of these statements? (p. 98).

Worship includes (1) the quickening of conscience by God's holiness; (2) the feeding of mind on His truth; (3) the purifying of imagination by His beauty; (4) the opening of the heart to His love; (5) the submission of the will to His purpose. What elements in public worship, as you are acquainted with it, serve these various activities? What alterations do you suggest to secure that the services of the Church should become more adequately the symbol and instrument of worship so defined? (p. 100).

And what can we do to bring our public worship into more effective relation with unemployment? (p. 101).

History is full of illustrations of the worshipping life transforming the world, and more full of illustrations of the actual Church losing opportunities to transform the world because it was not a true Church. Quote both kinds of illustrations, being careful to verify your references (p. 102).